Full-Stack Web Development

Building Scalable Web Apps with React and Node.js Create dynamic, real-world web applications with modern frameworks

THOMPSON CARTER

Table of Content

TABLE OF CONTENTS

Introduction

In today's fast-paced digital world, full-stack web development has become an essential skill for developers who want to build modern, dynamic, and scalable applications. With the advent of powerful JavaScript libraries like **React** and robust back-end technologies like **Node.js**, the ability to develop full-stack applications has never been more accessible. This book, *Full-Stack Web Development: Building Scalable Web Apps with React and Node.js*, is your comprehensive guide to mastering both the front-end and back-end aspects of web development, bringing everything together to help you build fully functional, real-world web applications.

Why Full-Stack Development?

Full-stack development refers to the practice of working with both the **front-end** (the client-side) and the **back-end** (the server-side) of a web application. As a full-stack developer, you are responsible for building the entire application—from the user interface (UI) to the server that handles business logic and data storage. By understanding both aspects of development, you gain the flexibility to create more cohesive applications and tackle problems across the entire software stack.

This book is designed for developers who are either new to full-stack development or looking to deepen their knowledge and expertise. With hands-on projects, real-world examples, and in-depth explanations, this book will guide you through the process of building scalable, secure, and efficient web applications.

What Will You Learn?

In this book, we'll explore the core technologies that make up the modern full-stack development stack—**React** for the front-end and **Node.js** for the back-end. By the end of this book, you will have a solid understanding of how to build full-stack web applications that leverage these powerful technologies.

1. **React for Front-End Development**: React is a JavaScript library developed by Facebook for building user interfaces. Its component-based architecture makes it easy to build reusable UI elements and manage application state efficiently. In this book, we will dive deep into React's core concepts, including:

   o **JSX** (JavaScript XML) for rendering components

   o **State and props** for managing data flow

   o **React Router** for client-side routing

   o **Context API** and **Redux** for state management

   o **Hooks** for functional components

2. **Node.js for Back-End Development**: Node.js is a JavaScript runtime built on Chrome's V8 engine that enables you to run JavaScript on the server-side. With Node.js, you can create fast, scalable network

applications. This book will guide you through the process of setting up a Node.js server, handling HTTP requests, integrating with databases like MongoDB, and building RESTful APIs. We'll also cover:

- o **Express.js** for creating APIs
- o **MongoDB** for data storage
- o **JWT (JSON Web Tokens)** for secure authentication
- o **Socket.io** for real-time communication

3. **Connecting the Front-End and Back-End**: One of the most important aspects of full-stack development is the interaction between the front-end and back-end. This book will teach you how to connect your React front-end to your Node.js back-end, allowing for seamless data flow between the user interface and the server. You'll learn how to:

- o Make API requests using **Axios** or **Fetch**
- o Use **Redux** for managing global state

- o Handle form submissions, authentication, and error handling
- o Implement real-time features with **WebSockets** (using Socket.io)

4. **Best Practices and Advanced Features**: As you gain more experience with full-stack development, you'll need to learn how to build scalable, maintainable applications. This book covers best practices and advanced features, such as:

- o **Code splitting** and **lazy loading** for better performance
- o **Server-side rendering (SSR)** with React for SEO optimization
- o **CI/CD** (Continuous Integration and Continuous Deployment) to automate the testing, building, and deployment process
- o Security, performance optimization, and strategies for scaling your application

5. **Final Project**: To bring everything together, we'll walk through a complete, hands-on project where you will build a real-world application—a **task management app**—from scratch. This project will help you apply everything you've learned in a practical, tangible way, from setting up the back-end and front-end to deploying the application to the web.

Who This Book is For

This book is aimed at developers who have some basic understanding of **JavaScript** and want to learn how to build full-stack applications using **React** and **Node.js**. Whether you are a beginner or have some experience with front-end or back-end development, this book is designed to guide you step by step through the entire process.

You should have basic knowledge of the following:

- HTML, CSS, and JavaScript

- Basic understanding of React (though no prior in-depth experience is necessary)

- Familiarity with using the command line and Git for version control

---

Why You Should Read This Book

Building full-stack web applications has become one of the most in-demand skills in software development today. The flexibility of working with both the client and server sides of an application enables you to take on more complex projects and create rich, interactive user experiences.

This book will equip you with:

- Practical skills to build **real-world applications** from scratch.

- A comprehensive understanding of **React**, **Node.js**, and how they work together to create full-stack applications.

- The tools to implement **advanced features** like real-time communication, secure authentication, and performance optimization.

- Best practices to make your applications scalable, maintainable, and secure.

By the end of this book, you'll have the skills to confidently build full-stack applications and be prepared to tackle more complex development challenges.

What's Inside the Book?

This book is divided into **18 chapters**, each focusing on different aspects of full-stack web development:

- **Chapters 1-4**: Set up and introduce React for front-end development.

- **Chapters 5-8**: Introduce Node.js, Express, and MongoDB for back-end development.

- **Chapters 9-12**: Focus on connecting the front-end and back-end, real-time communication, testing, debugging, and deploying your application.

- **Chapters 13-18**: Advanced features like Redux, code splitting, SSR, CI/CD pipelines, and a final full-stack project.

Each chapter builds upon the previous one, with clear explanations, examples, and exercises to reinforce key concepts. Whether you are building a personal project, developing a new feature for an existing app, or preparing for your next job as a full-stack developer, this book will provide the tools and knowledge you need to succeed.

The demand for **full-stack web developers** is growing rapidly as businesses and organizations need developers who can handle both the front-end and back-end of their applications. This book is designed to provide you with the knowledge and hands-on experience needed to build powerful, scalable, and user-friendly full-stack applications using **React** and **Node.js**.

By the end of this book, you'll be able to create applications that interact seamlessly with databases, offer real-time communication, and provide smooth user experiences across devices. Get ready to dive into the world of full-stack development and build your skills to the next level!

CHAPTER 1

INTRODUCTION TO FULL-STACK DEVELOPMENT

Overview of Full-Stack Development and the Key Roles in a Development Process

Full-stack development refers to the practice of working on both the front-end (client-side) and back-end (server-side) parts of a web application. A full-stack developer is responsible for building, testing, and maintaining the entire application, from the user interface (UI) to the database, ensuring that all components work together seamlessly.

The **front-end** is what users interact with directly. It involves building the user interface (UI) using languages like HTML, CSS, and JavaScript, along with libraries and frameworks like React. The **back-end** is the server-side part

15

of the application, where data is processed and stored, often built with languages like Node.js, Python, or Ruby.

Key roles involved in full-stack development include:

- **Front-End Developer**: Focuses on building the UI and implementing interactive features that users engage with. They work with HTML, CSS, JavaScript, and frameworks like React.

- **Back-End Developer**: Works on the server-side, databases, and APIs. They ensure that data is handled properly and securely, often using frameworks like Express.js or tools like MongoDB.

- **Full-Stack Developer**: A versatile developer who can handle both front-end and back-end development. They understand how all parts of a web application interact and work together to create a seamless experience.

- **DevOps Engineer**: Ensures that the software development process runs smoothly and efficiently, particularly in terms of deployment and maintenance.

- **UX/UI Designer**: Focuses on user experience (UX) and user interface (UI) design, ensuring that the application is visually appealing and user-friendly.

Introduction to React, Node.js, and How They Work Together

React and Node.js are two powerful technologies that make up the core of modern full-stack web development.

- **React**: A JavaScript library for building user interfaces. It is declarative, component-based, and efficient. React allows developers to create reusable components that manage their state and render UI based on that state. It has gained immense popularity due to its flexibility, high performance, and ease of integration with other libraries and frameworks. React's virtual DOM helps ensure that updates are efficient, providing a smooth user experience.

- **Node.js**: A runtime environment that enables developers to use JavaScript to write server-side code. Built on Chrome's V8 JavaScript engine, Node.js is highly efficient and perfect for building scalable network applications. With Node.js, developers can build the back-end logic, handle HTTP requests, interact with databases, and serve content to the front-end.

How They Work Together: React handles the front-end, where it interacts with users, while Node.js runs on the server, handling requests from React and interacting with databases or other services. The communication between the two happens through APIs (typically RESTful APIs or

GraphQL), where React sends HTTP requests to the server, and Node.js responds with the necessary data.

For example:

- React will request data (such as user information) from a Node.js server via an API.
- Node.js will query a database for that data, process it, and send it back to React.
- React will then render the data dynamically on the UI, providing a seamless experience for the user.

Importance of Scalability and Maintainability in Modern Web Applications

In modern web development, two key factors play a significant role in ensuring an application's long-term success: **scalability** and **maintainability**.

- **Scalability** refers to the ability of a web application to handle growth, whether it's an increase in the number of users, data, or overall traffic. As an app grows, it needs to be able to scale without compromising performance. Scalability is particularly important for applications that are expected to grow over time.

React helps with scalability on the front-end by promoting reusable components, allowing developers to add features without starting from scratch. It also helps by efficiently updating only parts of the page that need changing through its virtual DOM.

On the back-end, **Node.js** is highly scalable due to its non-blocking, event-driven architecture. This makes it ideal for building applications that need to handle a large number of simultaneous requests without slowing down.

- **Maintainability** ensures that the codebase remains manageable as the project evolves. This is achieved through clean code practices, documentation, and using frameworks and libraries that promote best practices.

React promotes maintainability by encouraging a component-based architecture, where each component encapsulates its own logic and state. This makes it easier to update or modify a part of the application without affecting the rest of the system.

On the server side, **Node.js** allows developers to use JavaScript across both the front-end and back-end, reducing the context-switching between different languages. The simplicity and lightweight nature of

Node.js contribute to cleaner, more maintainable code.

By focusing on scalability and maintainability, full-stack developers can create applications that not only perform well as they grow but are also easier to update and debug in the long run.

This chapter sets the foundation for understanding the core concepts behind full-stack development with React and Node.js. We've touched on the importance of these technologies in building scalable and maintainable applications, ensuring that you're well-prepared to dive deeper into each area throughout the book.

CHAPTER 2

SETTING UP YOUR DEVELOPMENT ENVIRONMENT

Installing Node.js and npm (Node Package Manager)

Before you can start building full-stack web applications, you need to set up your development environment. The first step in this process is installing **Node.js** and **npm** (Node Package Manager).

1. **Installing Node.js**:

   o Node.js is a runtime environment that allows you to run JavaScript code on the server-side. It includes npm, a package manager that makes it easy to install and manage dependencies (libraries and tools).

   o To install Node.js:

23

- Visit the official Node.js website: https://nodejs.org/

- Download the latest stable version (LTS) for your operating system (Windows, macOS, or Linux).

- Follow the installation instructions provided on the website.

After installation, verify that Node.js and npm are installed by running the following commands in your terminal (command prompt on Windows or terminal on macOS/Linux):

```bash
node -v
npm -v
```

This will display the installed versions of Node.js and npm, confirming that the installation was successful.

2. **Understanding npm**:

   ○ **npm** is the default package manager for Node.js. It helps you manage third-party libraries (called packages) that you will use in your application.

   ○ You can install packages globally or locally:

      ▪ **Globally**: Packages that you use across multiple projects (e.g., `npm install -g create-react-app`).

      ▪ **Locally**: Packages specific to a project (e.g., `npm install react`).

Setting Up a Code Editor (VS Code, Sublime Text, etc.)

To write and manage your code efficiently, you need a good code editor. The most popular code editor for JavaScript and web development is **Visual Studio Code (VS Code)**, but you can also use other editors like **Sublime Text** or **Atom**.

1. **Installing Visual Studio Code (VS Code)**:

o Visit the official Visual Studio Code website: https://code.visualstudio.com/

o Download and install the appropriate version for your operating system.

o After installation, open VS Code and customize it according to your needs (themes, fonts, etc.).

2. **Key Features of VS Code**:

o **IntelliSense**: Autocompletion for variables, functions, and methods, making coding faster and more efficient.

o **Integrated Terminal**: You can run your development commands directly from the editor.

o **Extensions**: VS Code supports a wide range of extensions, including ones for React, Node.js, debugging, and Git integration.

- Recommended extensions for React and Node.js:

  - **ESLint**: Linting for JavaScript code to ensure it follows best practices.

26

- **Prettier**: Automatic code formatting to maintain a consistent code style.

- **Reactjs code snippets**: Provides code snippets for faster React development.

- **Debugger for Chrome**: Debug your React app directly in the browser.

3. **Alternative Editors**:

   o **Sublime Text**: A lightweight editor that's fast and customizable. Ideal for those who prefer a simpler setup.

   o **Atom**: Developed by GitHub, it's another popular text editor with many customization options, including package support for React and Node.js.

Basic Tools and Libraries Needed for Development

As you develop your full-stack web applications with React and Node.js, you'll need a set of tools and libraries to streamline your workflow and improve your productivity.

1. **Webpack**: A powerful module bundler for JavaScript applications. Webpack bundles all your JavaScript files, CSS, and other assets into a single output file (or multiple files) to be served by the web browser.

   o To install Webpack, run:

   ```bash
   npm install --save-dev webpack webpack-cli
   ```

   o Webpack is highly configurable, and you'll likely need to set up a **webpack.config.js** file to define how your application should be bundled.

28

o Webpack can also help with tasks like:

- Transpiling modern JavaScript (using Babel).

- Bundling CSS and images.

- Setting up development servers.

2. **Babel**: Babel is a JavaScript compiler that lets you use the latest JavaScript features (ES6, ES7, etc.) without worrying about browser compatibility. Babel transpiles modern JavaScript into older syntax that works across all browsers.

o To install Babel, run:

```bash

npm install --save-dev @babel/core
@babel/preset-env @babel/cli
```

o You'll need a **.babelrc** file to configure Babel. Example:

```json
```

29

```
{

    "presets": ["@babel/preset-env"]

}
```

o Babel allows you to use features like arrow functions, template literals, and async/await without worrying about support in older browsers.

3. **React Development Tools**:

o **React DevTools**: A browser extension that helps you inspect and debug React applications. You can view the React component tree, inspect component states, and track performance.

   ▪ Install the React DevTools extension from Chrome Web Store or Firefox Add-ons.

4. **Other Libraries and Tools**:

o **Axios**: A popular library for making HTTP requests from React to your Node.js back-end.

   ▪ Install it with:

```bash
npm install axios
```

- o **React Router**: A library for managing navigation and routing in your React application.
  - Install it with:

```bash
npm install react-router-dom
```

- o **Nodemon**: A development tool for Node.js that automatically restarts the server when changes are detected in your code.
  - Install it globally with:

```bash
npm install -g nodemon
```

In this chapter, you've learned how to set up your development environment for building full-stack applications with React and Node.js. By installing Node.js and npm, setting up a powerful code editor like VS Code, and incorporating key development tools like Webpack, Babel, and others, you're ready to start building scalable and dynamic web applications. With these tools in place, you can begin writing efficient code and streamline your workflow as you progress in your development journey.

CHAPTER 3

INTRODUCTION TO HTML, CSS, AND JAVASCRIPT

HTML: Building the Structure of a Web Page

HTML (Hypertext Markup Language) is the standard language used to create the structure of web pages. It consists of a series of elements, or tags, that tell the web browser how to display content.

1. **Basic Structure of an HTML Document**: An HTML document starts with a `<!DOCTYPE>` declaration, followed by the `<html>` element that wraps all other content. Within the `<html>` element, the `<head>` and `<body>` elements serve different purposes:

- o   `<head>`: Contains meta-information about the document, such as the title, character encoding, and links to stylesheets.

- o   `<body>`: Contains the visible content of the web page, such as text, images, and other elements.

Here is a simple HTML structure:

html

```
<!DOCTYPE html>
<html lang="en">
  <head>
    <meta charset="UTF-8" />
    <meta                    name="viewport"
content="width=device-width,       initial-
scale=1.0" />
    <title>My First Web Page</title>
  </head>
  <body>
    <h1>Welcome to My Web Page!</h1>
    <p>This is a paragraph of text.</p>
```

34

```
<img src="image.jpg" alt="A beautiful
image" />
  </body>
</html>
```

2. **Key HTML Elements**:

   o **Headings**: `<h1>`, `<h2>`, `<h3>`, etc. – Used for defining headings, with `<h1>` being the most important.

   o **Paragraphs**: `<p>` – Used to define blocks of text.

   o **Images**: `<img>` – Used for embedding images in a page.

   o **Links**: `<a href="URL">` – Used for creating hyperlinks.

   o **Lists**: `<ul>` for unordered lists, `<ol>` for ordered lists, and `<li>` for list items.

3. **HTML Forms**: Forms are used to collect input from users. Common form elements include text fields, radio buttons, checkboxes, and submit buttons.

```
html
```

```
<form action="/submit" method="POST">
  <label for="name">Name:</label>
  <input type="text" id="name" name="name"
required />
  <button type="submit">Submit</button>
</form>
```

CSS: Styling Your Application for Responsiveness and User Experience

CSS (Cascading Style Sheets) is used to control the presentation of your HTML structure. It allows you to apply styles such as colors, fonts, spacing, and positioning, improving the look and feel of your web page.

1. **Basic CSS Syntax**: CSS follows a rule-based syntax, where each rule consists of a selector and a declaration block. The selector targets the HTML

element, while the declaration block contains property-value pairs.

css

```
h1 {
    color: blue;
    font-size: 24px;
}
```

In this example, the selector `h1` targets all `<h1>` elements, and the declaration block changes the text color to blue and the font size to 24px.

2. **Box Model**: The box model is the foundation of CSS layout. Every HTML element is represented as a rectangular box with the following parts:

   o **Content**: The actual content of the element (e.g., text or an image).

   o **Padding**: Space around the content, inside the border.

37

- o **Border**: A line surrounding the element.

- o **Margin**: Space outside the border, separating the element from others.

Example:

css

```
div {
  padding: 10px;
  border: 2px solid black;
  margin: 20px;
}
```

3. **Responsive Design**: Responsive design ensures that your web page looks good on all devices, from mobile phones to desktop computers. CSS media queries are used to apply different styles based on the screen size.

css

```
@media (max-width: 768px) {

  body {

    background-color: lightgray;

  }

}
```

4. **Flexbox and Grid Layouts**:

   o **Flexbox**: A one-dimensional layout system that allows items to be distributed in rows or columns with flexible spacing and alignment.

   css

```
.container {
    display: flex;
    justify-content: space-between;
}
```

   o **CSS Grid**: A two-dimensional layout system that allows you to create complex grid structures.

   css

39

```
.container {

  display: grid;

  grid-template-columns:    repeat(3,

1fr);

}
```

JavaScript: Adding Interactivity to Your Page

JavaScript is a programming language that allows you to add interactivity to your web pages. With JavaScript, you can handle user input, create dynamic content, and respond to user actions such as clicks, form submissions, and page loading.

1. **Basic JavaScript Syntax**: JavaScript uses variables, functions, and events to make the page interactive.

   o **Variables**: Used to store data.

   ```javascript
   let name = "John";
   ```

```
const age = 25;
```

o **Functions**: A block of code that performs a task when called.

```
javascript
```

```
function greet(name) {
  alert("Hello, " + name + "!");
}
greet("John");
```

2. **Event Handling**: JavaScript allows you to attach event listeners to elements, enabling the page to respond to user actions.

```
html
```

```
<button          onclick="alert('Button
clicked!')">Click me</button>
```

Or using JavaScript:

```
javascript
```

```javascript
document.getElementById("myButton").addEv
entListener("click", function() {
  alert("Button clicked!");
});
```

3. **DOM Manipulation**: The Document Object Model (DOM) represents the HTML structure of the page as a tree of objects. JavaScript allows you to interact with and modify the DOM dynamically.

```
javascript
```

```javascript
let           heading          =
document.querySelector("h1");
heading.textContent  =  "Welcome  to  My
Website!";
```

4. **AJAX and Fetch API**: The **AJAX** (Asynchronous JavaScript and XML) technique allows you to load content from the server without refreshing the page.

The modern **Fetch API** is a cleaner and more powerful way to make network requests.

```javascript
fetch('https://api.example.com/data')
  .then(response => response.json())
  .then(data => console.log(data));
```

In this chapter, you've learned the basics of **HTML, CSS,** and **JavaScript**, the three core technologies that form the backbone of web development.

- **HTML** provides the structure for web pages, defining content elements like headings, paragraphs, and forms.
- **CSS** enhances the look and feel of your website by styling elements, making the user interface visually appealing and responsive.

43

- **JavaScript** adds interactivity, allowing your web page to respond to user actions, load dynamic content, and manipulate the DOM.

Mastering these technologies is essential for building dynamic, modern web applications, and they will serve as the foundation for your journey into full-stack development.

CHAPTER 4

UNDERSTANDING REACT – THE BASICS

Introduction to React and Its Key Concepts (Components, JSX, Props, and State)

React is a popular JavaScript library used to build user interfaces, particularly for single-page applications (SPAs). It allows developers to create reusable UI components that are easy to manage, scale, and maintain. At its core, React is about building components that encapsulate both logic and appearance, which can then be reused throughout an application.

Here are the key concepts of React:

1. **Components**:

- o Components are the building blocks of a React application. They are self-contained units of functionality that can be reused throughout the application.

- o React components can be either **class-based** or **functional**, with functional components being the more common approach in modern React development.

- o Components can have two types: **Presentational Components** (which only handle the UI) and **Container Components** (which manage data and logic).

Example of a simple functional component:

```
javascript


function Welcome(props) {
  return <h1>Hello, {props.name}!</h1>;
}
```

2. **JSX (JavaScript XML)**:

46

- JSX is a syntax extension for JavaScript that allows you to write HTML-like code within your JavaScript. While React uses JavaScript, JSX makes it easier to define the structure of your UI in a way that looks very similar to HTML.

- JSX code is later compiled into regular JavaScript by tools like Babel.

Example of JSX:

```javascript
const element = <h1>Hello, world!</h1>;
```

3. **Props (Properties)**:

- **Props** are used to pass data from a parent component to a child component in React. They are read-only and help components communicate with each other.

47

o Props can be anything from a string or number to a function or array, and they make React components dynamic.

Example of using props:

javascript

```
function Greeting(props) {
  return <h1>Welcome, {props.user}!</h1>;
}


function App() {
  return <Greeting user="Alice" />;
}
```

4. **State**:

o **State** refers to data that changes over time and can affect how a component renders. Unlike props, which are passed down from parent to child, state is managed within a component itself.

    o   When state changes, React automatically re-renders the component to reflect the new state.

Example of using state in a class-based component:

```javascript
class Counter extends React.Component {
  constructor() {
    super();
    this.state = { count: 0 };
  }

  increment = () => {
    this.setState({                    count:
this.state.count + 1 });
  };

  render() {
    return (
      <div>
        <p>Count: {this.state.count}</p>
```

```
        <button

onClick={this.increment}>Increment</butto

n>

        </div>

      );

    }

  }
```

Creating Simple React Components and Understanding the Component Lifecycle

In React, you create components to manage the UI and logic of different parts of your application. Components can either be **functional** or **class-based**, and each has its own lifecycle.

1. **Functional Components**:

    o   Functional components are simpler and easier to write. They are just functions that take **props** as input and return JSX as output.

    Example of a functional component:

```javascript
```

```javascript
function Message(props) {
  return <h2>{props.text}</h2>;
}
```

2. **Class-based Components**:

- o   Class-based components are more powerful because they can manage state and have access to lifecycle methods.
- o   They are created using the `class` keyword and extend from `React.Component`.

Example of a class-based component:

```javascript
```

```javascript
class Hello extends React.Component {
  render() {
    return                    <h1>Hello,
{this.props.name}!</h1>;
  }
```

```
}
```

3. **Component Lifecycle**: React components go through several stages in their lifecycle, which can be managed through specific lifecycle methods. These methods allow you to perform actions at different points during a component's life (mounting, updating, unmounting).

   o **Mounting**: When a component is created and inserted into the DOM.

     ▪ `componentDidMount()`: Runs once after the component is added to the DOM. It is often used for fetching data or initializing libraries.

   o **Updating**: When a component's state or props change.

     ▪ `shouldComponentUpdate()`: Decides whether the component should re-render when state or props change.

- `componentDidUpdate()`: Runs after the component re-renders due to changes in state or props.

  o **Unmounting**: When a component is removed from the DOM.

    - `componentWillUnmount()`: Used to clean up resources, like canceling network requests or removing event listeners.

Introduction to React Hooks and Functional Components

React Hooks are a feature introduced in React 16.8 that allow you to use state and other React features without writing class components. Hooks make it easier to manage state, side effects, and other lifecycle events in functional components.

1. **useState Hook**:

- o The useState hook allows functional components to manage local state.
- o It returns an array with two elements: the current state value and a function to update it.

Example:

```javascript

import React, { useState } from 'react';

function Counter() {
  const [count, setCount] = useState(0);

  return (
    <div>
      <p>Count: {count}</p>
      <button onClick={() => setCount(count + 1)}>Increment</button>
    </div>
  );
}
```

54

2. **useEffect Hook**:

- o The `useEffect` hook is used for managing side effects in functional components, such as fetching data or subscribing to events.

- o It runs after the component renders and can be configured to run only once, when specific values change, or every time the component updates.

Example:

javascript

```javascript
import React, { useState, useEffect } from
'react';

function App() {
  const [data, setData] = useState([]);

  useEffect(() => {
    fetch('https://api.example.com/data')
      .then(response => response.json())
      .then(data => setData(data));
```

```
}, []); // Empty array means this effect
runs once after the initial render

    return (
      <div>
        <h1>Data</h1>
        <ul>
          {data.map(item => (
            <li
key={item.id}>{item.name}</li>
          ))}
        </ul>
      </div>
    );
}
```

3. **useContext Hook**:

   o The useContext hook allows you to access the
     context in your functional components, providing
     a simpler alternative to prop drilling.

Example:

```javascript
javascript


const UserContext = React.createContext();


function UserProfile() {
  const user = useContext(UserContext);


  return <h1>{user.name}</h1>;
}


function App() {
  const user = { name: 'John Doe' };


  return (
    <UserContext.Provider value={user}>
      <UserProfile />
    </UserContext.Provider>
  );
}
```

In this chapter, we explored the core concepts of React, including **components**, **JSX**, **props**, and **state**. We also looked at how to create simple React components and how React components interact with one another. By understanding React's **component lifecycle** and introducing **React Hooks**, you now have the tools to build dynamic, interactive applications using functional components. These are the foundational skills you'll need to create scalable React applications as you move forward in this book.

CHAPTER 5

BUILDING YOUR FIRST REACT APP

Setting Up a New React Project Using Create React App

To get started with React, you can use **Create React App** (CRA), a tool that sets up everything you need for a React project without needing to configure things manually. It handles the project setup, development server, and build tools.

1. **Install Node.js and npm** (if you haven't already): Before setting up a React project, ensure you have **Node.js** and **npm** installed. If not, follow the instructions from **Chapter 2** to install them.

2. **Create a New React App**:

o Open your terminal (command prompt on Windows or terminal on macOS/Linux) and run the following command to create a new React app:

bash

```
npx create-react-app my-app
```

o This will generate a new directory called my-app, where your React app will reside, and install all the necessary dependencies (like React, ReactDOM, and more).

3. **Start the Development Server**: After the installation is complete, navigate into the newly created project folder and run:

bash

```
cd my-app
npm start
```

    o   This will start the development server and open your application in the browser, typically at `http://localhost:3000`. You'll see the default React welcome page.

Now that the project is set up, you can begin building your app.

Structuring Components, Styling with CSS, and Routing with React Router

Once you've created your React app, it's time to add structure, style, and functionality.

1. **Structuring Components**:

    o   React applications are built using components. A well-structured React app follows a component-based approach, where each component encapsulates its own logic and layout.

- o Inside the `src` folder of your React project, you'll find an `App.js` file. This is the root component of your application.

Example of structuring components:

javascript

```
// src/components/Header.js
function Header() {
  return        <header><h1>My       React
App</h1></header>;
}


// src/components/Footer.js
function Footer() {
  return        <footer><p>©       2025      My
App</p></footer>;
}


// src/App.js
import Header from './components/Header';
```

```
import Footer from './components/Footer';

function App() {
  return (
    <div>
      <Header />
      <main>
        <h2>Welcome to my app!</h2>
      </main>
      <Footer />
    </div>
  );
}

export default App;
```

2. **Styling with CSS**: React allows you to style components using plain CSS, but you can also use CSS-in-JS solutions, such as styled-components. For now, let's stick with simple CSS.

63

o In the default CRA project, a `src/App.css` file is already included, which you can use to style your components.

o To style your components, simply import the CSS file in the relevant JavaScript file.

Example:

css

```css
/* src/App.css */
body {
  font-family: Arial, sans-serif;
  background-color: #f0f0f0;
}


header {
  background-color: #4CAF50;
  padding: 10px;
  text-align: center;
  color: white;
}
```

And then import the CSS file in App.js:

```
javascript
```

```
import './App.css';
```

3. **Routing with React Router**: To enable navigation within your React app, you'll need **React Router**. React Router allows you to create different views or pages and switch between them without reloading the page.

   o First, install React Router using npm:

   ```
   bash
   ```

   ```
   npm install react-router-dom
   ```

   o Next, set up routing in your app:

```
javascript
```

```
// src/components/Home.js
```

```
function Home() {

  return <h2>Home Page</h2>;

}


// src/components/About.js

function About() {

  return <h2>About Page</h2>;

}


// src/App.js

import { BrowserRouter as Router, Route,

Switch } from 'react-router-dom';

import Home from './components/Home';

import About from './components/About';

import Header from './components/Header';

import Footer from './components/Footer';

import './App.css';


function App() {

  return (

    <Router>

      <Header />
```

66

```
    <Switch>
        <Route        path="/"        exact
component={Home} />
        <Route                path="/about"
component={About} />
    </Switch>
    <Footer />
  </Router>
 );
}


export default App;
```

o The `<Switch>` component ensures that only one
   route is rendered at a time, and the `<Route>`
   component is used to define the path and the
   component it should render.

Connecting the Front-End with the Back-End (Fetching Data from a Server)

Now that you have a basic structure, it's time to connect the front-end with a back-end to make your app dynamic. In this section, we'll focus on **fetching data** from a server using **the Fetch API**.

1. **Setting Up a Sample Back-End (Optional)**: If you don't have a back-end yet, you can use a service like **JSONPlaceholder** (a free fake online REST API) to simulate fetching data. Alternatively, you can build a back-end using Node.js and Express, but for simplicity, we'll use JSONPlaceholder in this example.

2. **Fetching Data with the Fetch API**: React uses JavaScript's **Fetch API** to send HTTP requests to a server and retrieve data. You'll typically make these

requests inside the `useEffect` hook to fetch data when the component mounts.

Example of fetching data:

```javascript
import React, { useState, useEffect } from 'react';

function Posts() {
  const [posts, setPosts] = useState([]);

  useEffect(() => {

fetch('https://jsonplaceholder.typicode.com/posts')
      .then(response => response.json())
      .then(data => setPosts(data))
      .catch(error => console.error('Error fetching data:', error));
```

```
  }, []); // Empty dependency array means
it runs once when the component mounts


  return (
    <div>
      <h2>Posts</h2>
      <ul>
        {posts.map(post => (
          <li key={post.id}>
            <h3>{post.title}</h3>
            <p>{post.body}</p>
          </li>
        ))}
      </ul>
    </div>
  );
}


export default Posts;
```

In this example, the useEffect hook runs once when the component mounts. The fetch() function makes an HTTP GET request to the specified URL (`https://jsonplaceholder.typicode.com/post s`), and the response is parsed into JSON. The `setPosts` function updates the state with the fetched data, which is then rendered in the component.

3. **Using the Data in Your App**: Now, you can import and use the `Posts` component in your `App.js`:

```javascript
import React from 'react';
import Posts from './components/Posts';

function App() {
  return (
    <div>
      <h1>My React App</h1>
      <Posts />
    </div>
  );
```

```
    }


export default App;
```

In this chapter, we've built the foundation for your first React application. We covered:

- **Setting up a new React project** using Create React App.
- **Structuring components**, styling them with CSS, and enabling **routing** with React Router.
- **Connecting the front-end to the back-end** by fetching data from a server using the Fetch API.

By the end of this chapter, you've created a functional React app that can load and display data from an external source. This knowledge will serve as the foundation for building more complex React applications with dynamic content and advanced features.

CHAPTER 6

INTRODUCTION TO NODE.JS AND EXPRESS.JS

What is Node.js, and How Does It Work as a Server-Side Platform?

Node.js is a runtime environment that allows you to run JavaScript on the server-side. Traditionally, JavaScript was used for client-side programming (in the browser), but with Node.js, developers can now use JavaScript to build server-side applications as well. Node.js is built on **Chrome's V8 JavaScript engine**, which is known for its high performance, and it uses an **event-driven, non-blocking I/O model**. This makes Node.js particularly well-suited for building fast and scalable network applications, such as APIs and real-time applications.

1. **Asynchronous and Non-blocking**:

- o Node.js uses an **asynchronous** and **non-blocking** event loop to handle multiple requests without waiting for a response. This makes it highly efficient and suitable for I/O-heavy tasks, like reading files or making HTTP requests.

- o In traditional server-side programming, each request is handled sequentially, meaning the server waits for one request to finish before processing the next. However, with Node.js, when an I/O operation (such as a database query or file read) is requested, Node.js does not block the execution of other code. Instead, it moves on to the next task, and when the I/O operation finishes, it processes the result.

2. **Single-threaded**:

- o Node.js operates on a **single thread**, unlike traditional multi-threaded server-side technologies. This might sound like a limitation, but the asynchronous event-driven model compensates for this by handling many requests

74

concurrently without the need for creating multiple threads.

3. **Use Cases for Node.js**:

- o **Real-time applications** (e.g., chat applications, online gaming, collaboration tools).

- o **API servers** to serve RESTful services.

- o **Microservices** architectures where different services interact over HTTP.

- o **Streaming applications**, such as video or audio streaming, where large amounts of data need to be handled quickly and efficiently.

Introduction to Express.js as a Lightweight Framework for Building APIs

Express.js is a lightweight, fast, and minimalistic web application framework for Node.js. It simplifies the process of handling HTTP requests, managing routes, middleware, and rendering views. Express is designed to make it easier to create robust, scalable APIs by providing a set of utilities for common tasks in web development.

1. **Why Use Express.js?**

   o **Simplifies HTTP Requests**: Express provides an easy way to handle HTTP methods like GET, POST, PUT, and DELETE, and to manage request/response objects.

   o **Routing**: Express makes routing simple, allowing developers to define URL patterns and their associated handler functions (routes).

   o **Middleware**: Express allows you to add middleware functions to handle requests before they reach the final route handler. Middleware can be used for tasks like logging, authentication, error handling, and more.

   o **Extensible**: Express has a large ecosystem of third-party middleware, which makes adding features (such as security, database interactions, etc.) very easy.

2. **Setting Up Express**: To start using Express in a Node.js project, you need to install it via npm.

```bash
```

```
npm install express
```

3. **Key Features of Express.js**:

   o **Routing**: Defining how an application responds to HTTP requests at specific URL paths.

   o **Middleware**: Functions that process requests before they reach the route handler.

   o **Template Engines**: Express supports various template engines (such as EJS, Pug, etc.) to dynamically generate HTML views.

Setting Up Your First Express Server

Now that you understand what Node.js and Express are, let's create a simple Express server to handle basic HTTP requests.

1. **Creating Your Project Folder**:

   o Create a new directory for your Node.js project and navigate into it:

   bash

   ```
   mkdir my-express-app
   cd my-express-app
   ```

2. **Initializing the Project**:

   o Initialize a new Node.js project by running the following command. It will create a `package.json` file to manage dependencies:

   bash

78

```
npm init -y
```

3. **Installing Express**:

   o   Install the Express framework:

   ```
   bash
   ```

   ```
   npm install express
   ```

4. **Creating the Server**:

   o   In the root of the project, create a new file
   called `server.js`:

   ```
   bash
   ```

   ```
   touch server.js
   ```

   o   Open the `server.js` file and write the
   following code to create a basic Express
   server:

   ```
   javascript
   ```

79

```
const express = require('express');

const app = express();

const port = 3000;


// Middleware to handle incoming
requests
app.use(express.json());


// Route: Respond to GET request at
root URL
app.get('/', (req, res) => {

  res.send('Hello, World!');

});


// Route: Respond to GET request at
/api route
app.get('/api', (req, res) => {

  res.json({ message: 'Welcome to my
API!' });

});


// Start the server
```

```
app.listen(port, () => {

  console.log(`Server is running at

http://localhost:${port}`);

});
```

5. Understanding the Code:

- o **express()**: This creates an Express application.

- o **app.get()**: Defines a route that listens for GET requests. The first argument is the path, and the second is a callback function that handles the request and sends a response.

- o **app.listen()**: Starts the server and listens on the specified port (3000 in this case). When the server is running, it logs a message to the console.

6. Running the Server:

- o Start your server by running:

```bash
node server.js
```

- o You should see the message:

81

```
bash
```

```
Server        is        running        at
http://localhost:3000
```

7. **Testing the Server**:

   o Open a web browser or a tool like **Postman** and visit `http://localhost:3000`. You should see the message "Hello, World!".

   o If you visit `http://localhost:3000/api`, you should see a JSON response:

```
json
```

```
{ "message": "Welcome to my API!" }
```

In this chapter, we introduced **Node.js** as a server-side platform and discussed how it works, particularly its asynchronous and non-blocking architecture. We also explored **Express.js**, a lightweight framework that simplifies building APIs in Node.js.

By the end of this chapter, you have learned how to set up your first **Express server**, handle basic routes, and send responses to the client. With this foundation, you're now ready to expand your application by adding more routes, handling different HTTP methods, and integrating with databases. This marks the beginning of building powerful back-end services with Node.js and Express.

CHAPTER 7

BUILDING A RESTFUL API WITH NODE.JS AND EXPRESS

Creating Routes, Handling HTTP Requests (GET, POST, PUT, DELETE)

In this chapter, we'll dive into the process of building a **RESTful API** using **Node.js** and **Express.js**. A RESTful API is a standard way of designing networked applications to manage resources (data) using HTTP requests. We'll focus on handling four core HTTP methods: **GET**, **POST**, **PUT**, and **DELETE**, which correspond to the CRUD operations (Create, Read, Update, and Delete).

1. **Creating Routes**: In Express, routes define how your application responds to various HTTP requests.

Each route specifies a URL path and the HTTP method (GET, POST, etc.) to use for that request.

Example of a simple **GET** route:

```javascript
```

```javascript
app.get('/api/posts', (req, res) => {
  // Logic to fetch posts from a database
  res.json({ message: "List of all posts"
});
});
```

2. **Handling GET, POST, PUT, DELETE Requests**:

   Let's define routes for each HTTP method:

   o **GET**: Retrieve data from the server (Read operation).

   o **POST**: Send data to the server to create a new resource (Create operation).

   o **PUT**: Send data to update an existing resource (Update operation).

o **DELETE**: Remove a resource from the server (Delete operation).

Example code for a simple API that handles these HTTP methods:

```javascript
const express = require('express');
const app = express();
const port = 3000;

app.use(express.json()); // Middleware to
parse JSON request bodies

let posts = [
  { id: 1, title: 'First Post', content:
'This is my first post.' },
  { id: 2, title: 'Second Post', content:
'This is my second post.' }
];
```

86

```javascript
// GET: Fetch all posts
app.get('/api/posts', (req, res) => {
  res.json(posts);
});


// GET: Fetch a single post by ID
app.get('/api/posts/:id', (req, res) => {
  const post = posts.find(p => p.id ===
parseInt(req.params.id));
  if (!post) return res.status(404).json({
message: 'Post not found' });
  res.json(post);
});


// POST: Create a new post
app.post('/api/posts', (req, res) => {
  const newPost = {
    id: posts.length + 1,
    title: req.body.title,
    content: req.body.content
  };
  posts.push(newPost);
```

```
    res.status(201).json(newPost);          //
Respond with the newly created post
});


// PUT: Update an existing post
app.put('/api/posts/:id', (req, res) => {
    const post = posts.find(p => p.id ===
parseInt(req.params.id));
    if (!post) return res.status(404).json({
message: 'Post not found' });


    post.title = req.body.title;
    post.content = req.body.content;
    res.json(post);
});


// DELETE: Remove a post by ID
app.delete('/api/posts/:id', (req, res) =>
{
    const postIndex = posts.findIndex(p =>
p.id === parseInt(req.params.id));
```

```
if    (postIndex    ===    -1)    return
res.status(404).json({ message: 'Post not
found' });


  posts.splice(postIndex, 1); // Remove
the post
  res.json({ message: 'Post deleted' });
});


app.listen(port, () => {
  console.log(`Server     running     at
http://localhost:${port}`);
});
```

- o **GET** /api/posts: Fetches a list of all posts.

- o **GET** /api/posts/:id: Fetches a single post based on its id.

- o **POST** /api/posts: Creates a new post.

- o **PUT** /api/posts/:id: Updates an existing post by its id.

- o **DELETE** /api/posts/:id: Deletes a post by its id.

Using Middleware in Express.js

Middleware is a key concept in Express.js. It refers to functions that can process incoming requests before they reach the route handler or send a response to the client. Middleware can be used to handle tasks such as logging, authentication, body parsing, and more.

1. **Built-in Middleware**:

   o   `express.json()`: A built-in middleware that parses incoming JSON payloads in the request body.

   o   `express.static()`: A built-in middleware that serves static files, such as images or CSS files.

2. **Custom Middleware**: You can create your own middleware functions to perform specific tasks on incoming requests. For example, a middleware to log all incoming requests:

```javascript
app.use((req, res, next) => {
  console.log(`${req.method} request made
to: ${req.url}`);
  next(); // Pass the request to the next
middleware or route handler
});
```

3. **Using Middleware in Routes**: You can attach middleware to specific routes or apply it globally to all routes.

   o **Global Middleware**: Middleware applied to every request to the app.

   ```javascript
   app.use(express.json()); // Global
   middleware for parsing JSON
   ```

   o **Route-Specific Middleware**: Middleware applied only to a specific route.

```javascript
app.post('/api/posts', (req, res,
next) => {
  console.log('Request       body:',
req.body);
  next();
}, (req, res) => {
  const newPost = {
    id: posts.length + 1,
    title: req.body.title,
    content: req.body.content
  };
  posts.push(newPost);
  res.status(201).json(newPost);
});
```

Error Handling and Validation

Error handling and **input validation** are essential parts of building a robust API. You need to ensure that your API

92

responds appropriately to invalid requests and handles unexpected errors gracefully.

1. **Error Handling**: In Express, you can use custom error-handling middleware to catch errors that occur in your routes and handle them uniformly.

   Example of basic error handling:

   ```javascript
   app.use((req, res, next) => {
     const error = new Error('Not Found');
     error.status = 404;
     next(error); // Pass the error to the
   error-handling middleware
   });

   app.use((err, req, res, next) => {
     res.status(err.status || 500);
     res.json({
       message: err.message,
   ```

93

```
    error: err

  });

});
```

This code catches any errors that occur, sets the correct HTTP status code, and sends a JSON response with the error message and stack trace (if in development mode).

2. **Input Validation**: Validation ensures that the incoming data meets specific criteria before it is processed or stored. You can use a package like **Joi** or **express-validator** to simplify validation.

Example using **express-validator** to validate POST data:

```bash
bash
```

```
npm install express-validator
```

Then, in your route:

94

```javascript
const { body, validationResult } =
require('express-validator');


app.post('/api/posts', [


body('title').not().isEmpty().withMessage
('Title is required'),


body('content').not().isEmpty().withMessa
ge('Content is required')
], (req, res) => {
  const errors = validationResult(req);
  if (!errors.isEmpty()) {
    return res.status(400).json({ errors:
errors.array() });
  }


  const newPost = {
    id: posts.length + 1,
    title: req.body.title,
```

```
    content: req.body.content
  };
  posts.push(newPost);
  res.status(201).json(newPost);
});
```

This validation ensures that the `title` and `content` fields are not empty. If validation fails, it returns a `400 Bad Request` response with error details.

In this chapter, we have learned how to build a **RESTful API** using **Node.js** and **Express.js**. We covered:

- **Creating routes** and handling HTTP requests (GET, POST, PUT, DELETE).
- **Using middleware** to add functionality such as request logging and body parsing.

- **Error handling** and **input validation** to ensure that your API handles errors properly and only accepts valid data.

With these building blocks, you now have the foundation for building powerful, robust APIs that can serve data to your front-end applications or other consumers.

CHAPTER 8

WORKING WITH DATABASES (MONGODB)

Introduction to NoSQL Databases and MongoDB

Databases are crucial for storing and managing data in applications. While **relational databases** like MySQL and PostgreSQL organize data in tables and rows, **NoSQL databases** offer more flexibility in data storage by using various models such as document, key-value, column-family, and graph.

MongoDB is one of the most popular NoSQL databases. It stores data in a flexible, JSON-like format called **BSON** (Binary JSON), allowing for dynamic schema changes. Unlike relational databases, MongoDB does not require a predefined schema, meaning you can store different types of data in the same collection without worrying about compatibility.

Key Features of MongoDB:

- **Document-based storage**: Data is stored in documents (similar to JSON objects) in collections.
- **Scalability**: MongoDB can handle massive amounts of data and is easy to scale horizontally by adding more servers.
- **Flexible schema**: Each document in a collection can have a different structure, making it more flexible than relational databases.

Example of a MongoDB document:

```json
{
  "_id": ObjectId("5f50c31b62f51a0f4c6c5a2d"),
  "title": "My First Post",
  "content": "This is my first post in MongoDB.",
```

```
    "author": "John Doe"

}
```

Setting Up a MongoDB Database for Your Project

Before you can interact with MongoDB, you need to set up a MongoDB server or use a cloud service like **MongoDB Atlas**.

1. **Installing MongoDB Locally**:

    o   If you want to set up MongoDB locally, you can download and install it from the official MongoDB website: https://www.mongodb.com/try/download/comm unity.

    o   Follow the installation instructions for your operating system (Windows, macOS, or Linux).

2. **Using MongoDB Atlas** (Cloud Version):

o For convenience, you can also use **MongoDB Atlas**, a cloud-hosted MongoDB service. It offers free tiers and is great for small projects.

o Go to https://www.mongodb.com/cloud/atlas and sign up for a free account.

o Once logged in, create a new cluster and follow the instructions to connect to the cluster using MongoDB's connection string.

3. **Connecting to MongoDB from Node.js**:

o To interact with MongoDB from your Node.js application, you'll need to install the **MongoDB Node.js driver** or **Mongoose** (an Object Data Modeling (ODM) library for MongoDB).

Install Mongoose:

bash

```
npm install mongoose
```

Example code to connect to MongoDB:

```
javascript


const mongoose = require('mongoose');


mongoose.connect('mongodb://localhost:270
17/mydatabase', {
  useNewUrlParser: true,
  useUnifiedTopology: true
})
  .then(() => console.log('Connected  to
MongoDB'))
  .catch((error) => console.error('Could
not connect to MongoDB:', error));
```

- o Replace
  'mongodb://localhost:27017/mydataba
  se' with your own MongoDB connection string
  if using MongoDB Atlas or a different database.

CRUD Operations in MongoDB Using Mongoose

MongoDB supports **CRUD operations** (Create, Read, Update, and Delete) on documents. Mongoose simplifies working with MongoDB by providing a schema-based solution for data validation and interacting with the database.

1. **Setting Up a Mongoose Model**: First, define a **schema** that describes the structure of your documents, then create a **model** based on the schema to interact with the collection.

   Example of defining a schema and model for a **Post**:

   javascript

   ```
   const mongoose = require('mongoose');

   // Define a schema for a post
   const postSchema = new mongoose.Schema({
     title: {
       type: String,
   ```

```
    required: true

  },

  content: {

    type: String,

    required: true

  },

  author: String,

  createdAt: {

    type: Date,

    default: Date.now

  }

});


// Create a model based on the schema
const    Post    =    mongoose.model('Post',
postSchema);
```

2. **Create Operation (Insert Data)**: To insert a new document into a collection, you can use the `.save()` method on an instance of the model.

Example of creating a new post:

```javascript

const newPost = new Post({

  title: 'My Second Post',

  content: 'This is the content of my
second post.',

  author: 'Jane Doe'
});


newPost.save()

  .then((post) => {

    console.log('New     Post     Created:',
post);

  })

  .catch((error) => {

    console.error('Error creating post:',
error);

  });
```

3. **Read Operation (Fetch Data)**: To read or fetch data from the database, you can use methods like `.find()`, `.findOne()`, or `.findById()`.

105

Example of fetching all posts:

javascript

```
Post.find()
  .then((posts) => {
    console.log('All Posts:', posts);
  })
  .catch((error) => {
    console.error('Error fetching posts:',
error);
  });
```

Example of fetching a specific post by ID:

javascript

```
Post.findById('60d5e4f9e4b0d3f8e0d35a91')
  .then((post) => {
    if (!post) return console.log('Post
not found');
    console.log('Found Post:', post);
  })
```

```
.catch((error) => {

    console.error('Error fetching post:',
error);

    });
```

4. **Update Operation (Modify Data)**: To update existing documents, use the `.updateOne()`, `.updateMany()`, or `.findByIdAndUpdate()` methods.

Example of updating a post:

```
javascript
```

```
Post.findByIdAndUpdate('60d5e4f9e4b0d3f8e
0d35a91', {
    title: 'Updated Post Title'
}, { new: true })
    .then((updatedPost) => {
        console.log('Updated        Post:',
updatedPost);
    })
```

```
.catch((error) => {

    console.error('Error updating post:',
error);

    });
```

5. **Delete Operation (Remove Data)**: To delete documents, use methods like `.deleteOne()`, `.deleteMany()`, or `.findByIdAndDelete()`.

Example of deleting a post:

javascript

```
Post.findByIdAndDelete('60d5e4f9e4b0d3f8e
0d35a91')
  .then((deletedPost) => {
    console.log('Deleted          Post:',
deletedPost);
  })
  .catch((error) => {
    console.error('Error deleting post:',
error);
```

```
});
```

In this chapter, we introduced **MongoDB** and **Mongoose** as the primary tools for working with databases in a Node.js environment. We:

- Explored the concepts of **NoSQL databases** and how MongoDB stores data in a flexible, document-based format.

- Set up a MongoDB database and connected it to your Node.js project using **Mongoose**.

- Covered **CRUD operations** (Create, Read, Update, and Delete) in MongoDB using Mongoose models and methods.

Now, you have a solid foundation to integrate MongoDB into your full-stack applications, enabling dynamic data management for your projects.

109

CHAPTER 9

AUTHENTICATION AND AUTHORIZATION

Implementing User Authentication with JWT (JSON Web Tokens)

In this chapter, we will explore how to implement **authentication** and **authorization** in a Node.js application using **JWT (JSON Web Tokens)**. Authentication ensures that the user is who they say they are, while authorization determines whether a user has permission to perform a specific action.

JWT is a compact, URL-safe token that represents claims between two parties. It is commonly used for stateless authentication in web applications. JWT contains three parts: a **header**, a **payload**, and a **signature**.

1. **Why Use JWT?**

110

o **Stateless**: JWTs do not require storing session data on the server. This makes it ideal for scaling applications, as the server doesn't need to remember anything about the user between requests.

o **Secure**: JWTs are signed with a secret key, ensuring the integrity of the token and protecting it from tampering.

o **Compact**: JWTs are compact and can easily be passed through URLs, HTTP headers, or cookies.

2. **Installing Dependencies**: To implement JWT-based authentication, we need a few packages:

o `jsonwebtoken`: Library to sign and verify JWTs.

o `bcryptjs`: Library for hashing passwords.

Install the required dependencies:

```bash
bash
```

```
npm install jsonwebtoken bcryptjs
```

111

3. **Creating the Authentication Flow**:

   o **User Registration**: When a user registers, their password should be hashed using **bcryptjs**, and a JWT token should be generated and sent back to the client.

   o **User Login**: When a user logs in, the provided password should be compared with the hashed password stored in the database. If they match, a new JWT token is issued.

Here's how to implement this:

3.   **User Registration**:

```javascript
const bcrypt = require('bcryptjs');
const jwt = require('jsonwebtoken');
const express = require('express');
const User = require('./models/User'); // Assume User is a Mongoose model
```

```
const app = express();

app.use(express.json());


// Registration route

app.post('/register', async (req,
res) => {

  const { username, password } =
req.body;


  // Hash the password

  const hashedPassword = await
bcrypt.hash(password, 10);


  const newUser = new User({

    username,

    password: hashedPassword

  });


  try {

    await newUser.save();
```

```javascript
      res.status(201).send('User
registered');
  } catch (error) {
      res.status(400).json({    error:
'Registration failed' });
  }
});
```

4.   **User Login**:

```javascript
javascript

app.post('/login', async (req, res)
=> {
  const { username, password } =
req.body;

  // Find the user
  const user = await User.findOne({
username });
  if          (!user)          return
res.status(400).json({ error: 'User
not found' });
```

```
// Compare the password
const isMatch = await
bcrypt.compare(password,
user.password);
if (!isMatch) return
res.status(400).json({ error:
'Invalid password' });


// Create a JWT token
const token = jwt.sign({ userId:
user._id }, 'your-secret-key', {
expiresIn: '1h' });


// Send the token as a response
res.json({ token });
});
```

Protecting Routes with Authentication and Authorization Middleware

Once a user is authenticated, we need to protect certain routes so that only authenticated users can access them. We can achieve this by using **middleware** to check the validity of the JWT.

1. **Authentication Middleware**: This middleware will verify the token sent by the client (usually in the `Authorization` header) and ensure the user is authenticated.

   Example of authentication middleware:

   javascript

   ```javascript
   const jwt = require('jsonwebtoken');

   const authenticateToken = (req, res, next) => {
   ```

```
const               token               =
req.header('Authorization')?.split('
')[1]; // Assuming the token is sent as
'Bearer <token>'


   if            (!token)            return
res.status(403).json({   error:   'Access
denied' });


  try {
    const   decoded   =   jwt.verify(token,
'your-secret-key');
    req.user = decoded; // Attach the user
data to the request object
    next(); // Call the next middleware or
route handler
  } catch (error) {
    res.status(400).json({ error: 'Invalid
token' });
  }
};
```

2. **Authorization Middleware**: After authentication, you might want to restrict access to certain routes based on user roles or permissions (e.g., only admins can delete posts).

Example of role-based authorization middleware:

javascript

```
const authorizeAdmin = (req, res, next) =>
{
  if (req.user.role !== 'admin') {
    return res.status(403).json({ error:
'Access denied' });
  }
  next();
};
```

Now, you can use both middlewares to protect your routes. Here's an example of a protected route:

javascript

118

```
app.delete('/posts/:id',

authenticateToken, authorizeAdmin, (req,

res) => {

  // Logic to delete a post

  res.send('Post deleted');

});
```

Handling User Login and Registration in the Application

1. **User Registration Flow**:

    o   When a user registers, their password is hashed, and the data is stored in the database.

    o   After registration, a JWT token is generated and sent back to the user, allowing them to make authenticated requests.

2. **User Login Flow**:

    o   During login, the user sends their credentials (username and password) to the server.

119

o   The server verifies the password and, if valid, sends a JWT token back to the client.

o   The client stores the JWT token (typically in local storage or cookies) and includes it in the `Authorization` header of subsequent requests.

Example Flow for Authentication and Authorization

Here is a basic overview of the flow:

1. **User Registration**:

   o   **Request**: `POST /register`

   o   **Response**: Success message or error message

2. **User Login**:

   o   **Request**: `POST /login` (username and password in the request body)

   o   **Response**: JWT token if credentials are correct, or error message if not

3. **Accessing Protected Route**:

- o **Request**: Any route like `GET /profile` or `DELETE /posts/:id`

- o **JWT**: Sent in the `Authorization` header as `Bearer <token>`

- o **Response**: Data or success if token is valid, or an error message if token is invalid

---

In this chapter, we've learned how to implement **authentication** and **authorization** in a Node.js application using **JWT**. Here's what we covered:

- **User authentication** using JWT for secure login and registration.

- **JWT middleware** to protect routes and ensure only authenticated users can access them.

- **Role-based authorization** to restrict access to certain routes based on user roles.

- Handling user login and registration to enable users to authenticate and access protected resources.

With this knowledge, you can add secure user authentication to your Node.js applications, making them safe and accessible only to authorized users.

CHAPTER 10

CONNECTING REACT WITH NODE.JS (FRONTEND AND BACKEND INTEGRATION)

Fetching Data from Your Node.js API into Your React Components

To build dynamic and interactive applications, you'll often need to connect the **front-end** (React) with the **back-end** (Node.js API). The back-end serves as the data provider, while the front-end fetches this data and displays it to the user. This chapter will focus on how to connect your React app with your Node.js API and manage the data flow.

Let's start by making an API call from React to your Node.js back-end to fetch data.

1. **Creating the Node.js API**: For simplicity, let's assume we have a basic Node.js API running with

123

Express.js that returns a list of posts. Here's an example:

javascript

```
// server.js (Node.js API)
const express = require('express');
const app = express();
const port = 3000;

// Mock data
const posts = [
  { id: 1, title: 'Post One', content:
'This is the first post' },
  { id: 2, title: 'Post Two', content:
'This is the second post' },
];

app.get('/api/posts', (req, res) => {
  res.json(posts);
});
```

```
app.listen(port, () => {

    console.log(`Server       running       at

http://localhost:${port}`);

});
```

2. **Fetching Data from React**: In your React application, you will fetch this data from the back-end API and render it in your components.

   o You can fetch data using **Axios** or the native **Fetch API**. Both are commonly used in React applications to make HTTP requests.

Using Axios or Fetch for Making API Requests

1. **Using Axios**: **Axios** is a promise-based HTTP client that simplifies the process of making HTTP requests. It automatically transforms JSON data and supports features like request cancellation and interceptors.

   First, you need to install **Axios**:

```
bash
```

```
npm install axios
```

Then, you can use Axios to fetch data from your Node.js API:

```
javascript
```

```javascript
import React, { useState, useEffect } from
'react';
import axios from 'axios';

function PostList() {
  const [posts, setPosts] = useState([]);

  useEffect(() => {

axios.get('http://localhost:3000/api/post
s')
      .then((response) => {
        setPosts(response.data);
      })
```

126

```
        .catch((error) => {

            console.error('There was an error

fetching the posts!', error);

        });

    }, []);


    return (

      <div>

        <h1>Posts</h1>

        <ul>

          {posts.map(post => (

            <li key={post.id}>

              <h2>{post.title}</h2>

              <p>{post.content}</p>

            </li>

          ))}

        </ul>

      </div>

    );

}


export default PostList;
```

o In this example, `useEffect` is used to fetch the data when the component mounts.

o The `axios.get()` function makes a GET request to the Node.js API and updates the `posts` state with the fetched data.

2. **Using Fetch API**: The **Fetch API** is built into modern browsers and can be used to make HTTP requests. It is also promise-based and is widely supported in React applications.

Example using **Fetch**:

```javascript
```

```javascript
import React, { useState, useEffect } from 'react';

function PostList() {
  const [posts, setPosts] = useState([]);

  useEffect(() => {
```

```
fetch('http://localhost:3000/api/posts')

    .then(response => response.json())

    .then(data => setPosts(data))

    .catch(error => {

        console.error('There was an error
fetching the posts!', error);

    });

}, []);


    return (

      <div>

        <h1>Posts</h1>

        <ul>

          {posts.map(post => (

            <li key={post.id}>

              <h2>{post.title}</h2>

              <p>{post.content}</p>

            </li>

          ))}

        </ul>

      </div>
```

129

```
    );

}
```

```
export default PostList;
```

- o Here, `fetch()` is used to make the GET request, and the response is parsed as JSON before setting the state.

Managing Data with React's State and Context API

Once you fetch data from your back-end API, you need to manage and pass it around your React components. React provides a few ways to manage state, and we'll cover two of the most common approaches: **local component state** and **React Context API**.

1. **Using Component State**: In the examples above, we used **local state** in the `PostList` component to store and display the fetched data. The `useState` hook

allows you to manage local state, and you can update it when new data is fetched.

This is perfect for scenarios where you only need to manage the state locally within one component.

2. **Using React Context API**: If you have data that needs to be accessed by multiple components throughout your app, you can use the **Context API**. The Context API allows you to share state globally without passing props down manually at every level.

Example of setting up **Context API** to manage posts data:

1. **Creating the Context**:

```javascript
import React, { createContext,
useState, useEffect } from 'react';
```

```
const PostContext = createContext();

function PostProvider({ children })
{
  const [posts, setPosts] =
useState([]);

  useEffect(() => {

fetch('http://localhost:3000/api/po
sts')
      .then((response)            =>
response.json())
      .then((data)                =>
setPosts(data))
      .catch((error)              =>
console.error('Error        fetching
posts:', error));
  }, []);

  return (
```

```
<PostContext.Provider    value={{
posts }}>

    {children}

    </PostContext.Provider>

  );

}


export { PostProvider, PostContext
};
```

- Here, we created a `PostContext` to provide the posts data and wrapped the entire application with the `PostProvider`.

2. **Consuming the Context**: To access the posts in any component, you use the `useContext` hook:

```
javascript
```

```
import React, { useContext } from 'react';
```

```
import { PostContext } from
'./PostProvider';

function PostList() {
  const { posts } =
useContext(PostContext);

  return (
    <div>
      <h1>Posts</h1>
      <ul>
        {posts.map((post) => (
          <li key={post.id}>
            <h2>{post.title}</h2>
            <p>{post.content}</p>
          </li>
        ))}
      </ul>
    </div>
  );
}
```

134

```
export default PostList;
```

- The `useContext` hook accesses the global `posts` state provided by the `PostProvider`. Now, any component within the provider can access the posts data without needing to pass it down as props.

In this chapter, we've learned how to connect your **React front-end** with your **Node.js back-end** to fetch data and manage it effectively. Here's a summary of the key points covered:

- **Fetching data** from a Node.js API into React components using **Axios** or **Fetch**.
- Using **React's state** to store and manage the fetched data locally within a component.

135

- Using **React Context API** for managing global state when multiple components need to access the same data.

By mastering these concepts, you can build full-stack applications where your front-end and back-end work seamlessly together, enabling dynamic and data-driven user experiences.

CHAPTER 11

BUILDING REAL-WORLD FEATURES – USER PROFILES AND FORMS

Creating Dynamic Forms in React (Using Controlled Components)

Forms are an essential part of modern web applications, allowing users to input data, submit it, and interact with the back-end. In React, forms are typically created using **controlled components**, where the form elements' state is managed by React. This allows for real-time updates and validation.

1. **Controlled Components**: A controlled component is a form element where React manages the state. This means the value of the input is bound to the

component's state, and any changes to the input trigger a state update.

Example of a controlled input field:

javascript

```
import React, { useState } from 'react';

function UserForm() {
  const [name, setName] = useState('');
  const [email, setEmail] = useState('');

  const handleNameChange = (e) => {
    setName(e.target.value);
  };


  const handleEmailChange = (e) => {
    setEmail(e.target.value);
  };


  const handleSubmit = (e) => {
```

138

```
    e.preventDefault();

    console.log('Form Submitted:', { name,
email });

  };


  return (
    <form onSubmit={handleSubmit}>
      <label>
        Name:
        <input  type="text"  value={name}
onChange={handleNameChange} />
      </label>
      <br />
      <label>
        Email:
        <input type="email" value={email}
onChange={handleEmailChange} />
      </label>
      <br />
      <button
type="submit">Submit</button>
    </form>
```

```
    );

}
```

```
export default UserForm;
```

In this example:

- o value attributes bind the inputs to React's state (name and email).

- o onChange handlers update the state whenever the user types into the input fields.

Handling Form Submissions and Validation

Handling form submissions and performing validation are crucial parts of user interaction. Here, we'll cover how to handle form submissions and perform basic client-side validation.

1. **Form Submission**: When the user submits a form, the form data is collected, validated, and then sent to

the back-end for processing (e.g., saving to the database).

Example of handling a form submission:

javascript

```javascript
const handleSubmit = (e) => {
  e.preventDefault();   // Prevent the default form submission

  // Validate input fields before submitting
  if (!name || !email) {
    alert('All fields are required');
    return;
  }

  console.log('Form Submitted:', { name, email });
  // Send data to the back-end (e.g., using Axios or Fetch)
```

141

```
};
```

In the example, before sending the form data, we check if both the `name` and `email` fields are filled. If they are empty, an alert is shown, and the form is not submitted.

2. **Client-Side Validation**: Client-side validation ensures that the data entered by the user is in the correct format before submission. You can validate using regular expressions, custom checks, or HTML5 form validation.

Example of validating an email:

```javascript
const handleSubmit = (e) => {
  e.preventDefault();

  if (!name || !email) {
    alert('All fields are required');
```

```
    return;

  }


  const emailPattern = /^[a-zA-Z0-9._%+-
]+@[a-zA-Z0-9.-]+\.[a-zA-Z]{2,}$/;
  if (!emailPattern.test(email)) {
    alert('Please enter a valid email
address');
    return;
  }


  console.log('Form Submitted:', { name,
email });
  // Submit the form data
};
```

In this example, we use a regular expression to validate that the entered email matches the standard email format.

Building a User Profile Page and Integrating it with Your Node.js

Back-End

User profiles are a core feature in many applications, allowing users to view and update their personal information. In this section, we'll discuss how to create a user profile page and integrate it with your Node.js back-end.

1. **Creating the User Profile Page in React**: The user profile page will display the user's information and allow them to update it.

   Example of a user profile component:

   ```javascript
   import React, { useState, useEffect } from 'react';
   import axios from 'axios';

   function UserProfile() {
     const [user, setUser] = useState({});
   ```

144

```
  const    [editMode,    setEditMode]    =
useState(false);
  const [name, setName] = useState('');
  const [email, setEmail] = useState('');


  useEffect(() => {
    // Fetch user data from the API when
the component mounts

axios.get('http://localhost:3000/api/user
')
      .then((response) => {
        setUser(response.data);
        setName(response.data.name);
        setEmail(response.data.email);
      })
      .catch((error) => {
        console.error('Error fetching user
data:', error);
      });
  }, []);
```

145

```
const handleSubmit = (e) => {

  e.preventDefault();

  // Update the user profile data on the
server

axios.put('http://localhost:3000/api/user
', { name, email })

    .then((response) => {

      setUser(response.data);

      setEditMode(false); // Exit edit
mode after successful update

    })

    .catch((error) => {

      console.error('Error      updating
profile:', error);

    });

};


return (

  <div>

    <h1>User Profile</h1>

    {editMode ? (
```

146

```jsx
<form onSubmit={handleSubmit}>
  <label>
    Name:
    <input type="text"
    value={name} onChange={(e) =>
    setName(e.target.value)} />
  </label>
  <br />
  <label>
    Email:
    <input type="email"
    value={email} onChange={(e) =>
    setEmail(e.target.value)} />
  </label>
  <br />
  <button type="submit">Save
Changes</button>
    <button type="button"
onClick={() =>
setEditMode(false)}>Cancel</button>
</form>
) : (
```

147

```
    <div>

        <p><strong>Name:</strong>

{user.name}</p>

        <p><strong>Email:</strong>

{user.email}</p>

        <button    onClick={()    =>

setEditMode(true)}>Edit Profile</button>

    </div>

  )}

  </div>

 );

}


export default UserProfile;
```

In this component:

- o We fetch the user's data from the API when the component mounts using `axios`.
- o The user can switch between viewing and editing their profile using the `editMode` state.

    o   When the user submits the form, their profile data is updated via a PUT request to the back-end API.

2. **Setting Up the Back-End for User Profile Management**: On the Node.js back-end, we need to handle fetching and updating the user's profile.

Example of setting up the back-end routes:

```javascript
const express = require('express');
const app = express();
const port = 3000;

app.use(express.json());

let user = {
  name: 'John Doe',
  email: 'john@example.com'
};

// GET: Fetch user profile
```

```
app.get('/api/user', (req, res) => {
  res.json(user);
});


// PUT: Update user profile
app.put('/api/user', (req, res) => {
  const { name, email } = req.body;
  if (name) user.name = name;
  if (email) user.email = email;
  res.json(user);
});


app.listen(port, () => {
  console.log(`Server      running      at
http://localhost:${port}`);
});
```

In this example:

- o The GET /api/user route returns the current
  user profile.

- o The `PUT /api/user` route updates the user's name and email based on the data sent in the request body.

In this chapter, we learned how to build real-world features such as **user profiles** and **forms** in a React application. Here's a recap of what we covered:

- **Creating dynamic forms** using controlled components in React.

- **Handling form submissions** and performing basic **client-side validation**.

- **Building a user profile page** that allows users to view and update their profile.

- **Integrating the React front-end** with a **Node.js back-end** to fetch and update user data.

151

These concepts are essential for building interactive and dynamic user interfaces in modern web applications. By combining front-end React components with a back-end API, you can create rich, full-stack applications that provide seamless user experiences.

CHAPTER 12

BUILDING SCALABLE APPLICATIONS WITH REACT AND NODE.JS

Optimizing Your React Components for Scalability

When building large-scale applications with React, scalability is key. Optimizing your React components for scalability ensures that your app remains performant, maintainable, and easy to expand over time. Below are a few techniques and best practices for achieving scalability in React.

1. **Component Reusability and Modularity**: One of the core principles of React is building **reusable components**. To maintain scalability, keep components small, focused, and modular. Each

component should handle a specific part of your UI and have a single responsibility.

Example:

javascript

```
function Button({ label, onClick }) {
  return                        <button
onClick={onClick}>{label}</button>;
}


// Usage in other components
<Button                   label="Submit"
onClick={handleSubmit} />
```

By breaking down the UI into small, reusable components, you can easily scale the application and reuse components across different parts of the application.

154

2. **Lazy Loading and Code Splitting**: As your React application grows, the bundle size will increase, affecting performance. **Lazy loading** helps by loading components only when they are needed, improving initial load time. React's **React.lazy** and **Suspense** make it easy to implement lazy loading.

Example:

```javascript
import React, { Suspense } from 'react';

const LazyComponent = React.lazy(() =>
import('./LazyComponent'));

function App() {
  return (
    <div>
      <Suspense
fallback={<div>Loading...</div>}>
```

```
        <LazyComponent />

    </Suspense>

  </div>

);

}
```

Code splitting breaks the application into smaller chunks that are loaded only when necessary. Tools like **Webpack** can help automatically split your code into smaller bundles.

3. **State Management**: As applications scale, managing state across many components can become difficult. Instead of passing props down to multiple layers, use **state management libraries** like **Redux**, **Context API**, or **Recoil** to centralize and manage your app's state. This avoids prop drilling and makes it easier to share state across components.

Example with **Context API**:

```javascript

const AppContext = React.createContext();

function AppProvider({ children }) {
  const [user, setUser] = useState(null);

  return (
    <AppContext.Provider value={{ user,
setUser }}>
      {children}
    </AppContext.Provider>
  );
}

function UserProfile() {
  const { user } = useContext(AppContext);
  return <div>{user ? `Hello,
${user.name}` : 'No user logged in'}</div>;
}
```

157

4. **Optimizing Re-renders**: As your application grows, excessive re-renders can affect performance. Use **React.memo** to prevent unnecessary re-renders of functional components and **useMemo** and **useCallback** hooks to optimize computationally expensive calculations and function declarations.

Example:

```javascript
const MemoizedComponent = React.memo(({
name }) => {
  return <div>{name}</div>;
});


// useMemo to optimize calculations
const memoizedValue = useMemo(() =>
computeExpensiveValue(input), [input]);


// useCallback to memoize functions
```

```
const memoizedCallback = useCallback(() =>
{
  console.log('Callback function');
}, []);
```

Best Practices for Handling Large-Scale Applications

As your React application grows, it becomes more important to follow best practices that keep the codebase manageable and maintainable.

1. **Folder Structure**: A well-organized folder structure can make your application easier to navigate as it scales. There is no one-size-fits-all solution, but a commonly used structure is:

bash

```
src/
  components/      # Reusable components
```

159

```
    pages/              # Components tied to
routes or views
    services/           # API calls, utilities,
and business logic
    store/              # State management (e.g.,
Redux, Context)
    assets/             # Images, fonts, etc.
    styles/             # Global CSS or styled-
components
    hooks/              # Custom hooks
```

This structure makes it clear where each part of the application lives, which will make it easier to scale.

2. **Error Boundaries**: In large applications, errors can happen at any point. **Error boundaries** are React components that catch JavaScript errors in their child components, log the errors, and display a fallback UI. This can prevent the entire app from crashing.

Example of an error boundary:

160

```javascript
class ErrorBoundary extends React.Component {
  constructor(props) {
    super(props);
    this.state = { hasError: false };
  }

  static getDerivedStateFromError(error) {
    return { hasError: true };
  }

  componentDidCatch(error, info) {
    console.log(error, info);
  }

  render() {
    if (this.state.hasError) {
      return <h1>Something went wrong.</h1>;
    }
```

```
    return this.props.children;

  }

}


// Usage
<ErrorBoundary>
  <MyComponent />
</ErrorBoundary>
```

3. **Testing**: As applications grow, testing becomes essential to ensure everything works as expected. Tools like **Jest**, **React Testing Library**, and **Cypress** can help with unit testing, integration testing, and end-to-end testing.

   Example using **React Testing Library**:

```javascript
import { render, screen } from '@testing-library/react';
import UserProfile from './UserProfile';
```

```
test('displays user profile', () => {

  render(<UserProfile />);

  const            linkElement          =
  screen.getByText(/hello/i);


  expect(linkElement).toBeInTheDocument();
});
```

4. **API Design**: Design your API in a way that is consistent, scalable, and easy to consume by the front-end. Follow RESTful conventions or consider using **GraphQL** if your application requires flexible queries. Ensure your API can scale by handling requests efficiently, implementing pagination for large datasets, and leveraging caching when possible.

Techniques for Structuring Your Node.js Server and React Front-End for Scalability

As both the front-end and back-end of your application grow, structuring them for scalability is crucial. This involves organizing both the **React** app and the **Node.js server** in a way that ensures they can grow independently without creating bottlenecks.

1. **Node.js Server Structure**: A scalable Node.js server should be modular, where each module is responsible for a specific functionality, such as authentication, database interaction, or routing.

   Example folder structure for a Node.js API:

   ```bash
   server/
     controllers/      # Functions for handling HTTP requests
   ```

```
routes/              # Routes for different
API endpoints
models/              # Database models (e.g.,
Mongoose models)
services/            # Business logic and
data services
middleware/          # Authentication,
validation, etc.
config/              # Configuration files
(e.g., environment variables)
```

2. **Handling Large-Scale APIs**:

   o **Use of asynchronous programming**: Node.js is inherently asynchronous, but it's important to leverage this feature when building scalable APIs. Use async/await, promises, and non-blocking operations to prevent the server from being blocked during I/O operations (e.g., database queries).

   o **Clustering**: In high-traffic environments, consider using **Node.js clustering** to take advantage of multi-core systems. The `cluster` module allows you to create child processes (workers) that share the same server port, making it possible to handle more requests.

3. **Frontend-Backend Separation**: For scalability, it's beneficial to keep the **front-end** and **back-end** codebases separate. This allows the teams to work independently, scale resources (e.g., load balancing for APIs), and deploy them separately. You can use **proxying** in the development environment (e.g., through Webpack or Create React App) to interact with the API while keeping them separated in production.

Example (React proxy setup): In your React app, add a proxy to the `package.json` file to forward requests to the Node.js API:

```
json
```

166

```
"proxy": "http://localhost:3000"
```

4. **CDN and Static Assets**: For performance and scalability, host static assets (images, CSS, JavaScript files) using a **Content Delivery Network (CDN)**. This reduces load on your server and speeds up the delivery of assets by caching them at multiple locations worldwide.

In this chapter, we covered techniques for building **scalable applications** using **React** and **Node.js**. We discussed:

- **Optimizing React components** for scalability, including reusability, lazy loading, and state management.
- Best practices for handling **large-scale applications**, such as organizing your project structure, error handling, testing, and API design.

- Techniques for structuring both your **Node.js server** and **React front-end** for scalability, focusing on modularity, API efficiency, and separation of concerns.

By following these guidelines and practices, you can ensure that your applications are well-architected to handle growth and can easily scale with increasing complexity and traffic.

CHAPTER 13

REAL-TIME COMMUNICATION WITH WEBSOCKETS

Introduction to WebSockets and Real-Time Data Exchange

In many modern web applications, users expect immediate feedback, such as live notifications, real-time updates, or chat messages. For these features, traditional request-response communication via HTTP is often insufficient because it doesn't allow the server to push data to the client without the client making a new request.

WebSockets solve this problem by establishing a persistent, full-duplex communication channel between the client and server. Unlike HTTP, WebSockets allow the server to send data to the client at any time, providing true **real-time communication**.

169

1. **What is WebSocket?** WebSocket is a protocol that enables two-way communication between the client and server over a single, long-lived connection. Once the connection is established, both the server and the client can send data back and forth without having to repeatedly establish new connections.

2. **Why Use WebSockets?**

   o **Low latency**: Since the connection is persistent, WebSockets provide faster communication as there's no need to repeatedly open new connections.

   o **Real-time interaction**: Perfect for applications that require live data, such as chat apps, notifications, live updates, and collaborative tools.

   o **Efficient**: WebSockets use much less overhead compared to traditional HTTP polling or long polling.

Implementing WebSockets with Socket.io in Both React and Node.js

While WebSockets provide the protocol for real-time communication, using **Socket.io** makes it easier to implement WebSockets in a JavaScript environment. Socket.io is a popular library that provides WebSocket-like functionality, even supporting fallback options for browsers that don't support WebSockets natively.

1. **Setting Up Socket.io in Node.js**: First, you need to install **Socket.io** on the server (Node.js side) to handle WebSocket communication.

   To install the necessary packages:

   ```bash
   npm install socket.io
   ```

Here's how to set up a basic **Node.js server** with **Socket.io**:

javascript

```javascript
const express = require('express');
const http = require('http');
const socketIo = require('socket.io');

const app = express();
const server = http.createServer(app);
const io = socketIo(server);

// Set up a basic route
app.get('/', (req, res) => {
  res.send('Socket.io server running');
});

// WebSocket connection handler
io.on('connection', (socket) => {
  console.log('New client connected');
```

```
// Listen for 'chat message' event from
the client
  socket.on('chat message', (msg) => {
    console.log('Message received: ' +
msg);
    // Emit the message to all connected
clients
    io.emit('chat message', msg);
  });


  // Handle client disconnection
  socket.on('disconnect', () => {
    console.log('Client disconnected');
  });
});

const port = 3000;
server.listen(port, () => {
  console.log(`Server        running        on
http://localhost:${port}`);
});
```

In this example:

- o `socket.on('connection')` listens for incoming connections from clients.

- o `socket.on('chat message')` listens for events emitted from the client (in this case, chat messages).

- o `io.emit('chat message')` sends the message to all connected clients.

2. **Setting Up Socket.io in React**: On the client-side, you need to install the **Socket.io client** to interact with the WebSocket server. To install the client-side library:

```bash
bash
```

```bash
npm install socket.io-client
```

Here's how to set up **Socket.io** in a **React component** to send and receive real-time messages:

```javascript
javascript
```

174

```
import React, { useState, useEffect } from
'react';

import io from 'socket.io-client';


const           socket           =
io('http://localhost:3000');


function ChatApp() {
   const    [message,    setMessage]    =
useState('');
   const    [messages,    setMessages]    =
useState([]);


   // Listen for incoming messages from the
server
   useEffect(() => {
      socket.on('chat message', (msg) => {
         setMessages((prevMessages)           =>
[...prevMessages, msg]);
      });
```

```
    // Clean up the listener when the
component unmounts
    return () => {
      socket.off('chat message');
    };
  }, []);


  const handleSendMessage = (e) => {
    e.preventDefault();
    if (message.trim()) {
      socket.emit('chat          message',
message);  // Emit message to the server
      setMessage('');
    }
  };


  return (
    <div>
      <h2>Real-Time Chat</h2>
      <ul>
        {messages.map((msg, index) => (
          <li key={index}>{msg}</li>
```

176

```
      ) ) }

    </ul>

    <form onSubmit={handleSendMessage}>

      <input

        type="text"

        value={message}

        onChange={ (e)                        =>
setMessage(e.target.value) }

        placeholder="Type your message"

      />

      <button
type="submit">Send</button>

    </form>

  </div>

  );

}


export default ChatApp;
```

In this React component:

o `socket.on('chat message')` listens for incoming messages from the server and updates the state with new messages.

o `socket.emit('chat message')` sends the chat message from the client to the server when the user submits the form.

Use Cases: Building a Real-Time Chat Application

Now that we've set up WebSocket communication with Socket.io, let's explore how to apply this to a real-world use case: a **real-time chat application**.

1. **Core Features of a Real-Time Chat App**:

   o **User Authentication**: Users should be able to log in to the app and start sending messages.

   o **Real-time Messaging**: Messages should appear instantly on all users' screens without needing to refresh the page.

- o **Message History**: A history of past messages should be available when users reconnect.

- o **Multiple Rooms/Channels**: Users can join different chat rooms or channels and exchange messages specific to those rooms.

2. **Extending the Basic Chat App**: To make the chat app more complex and realistic, we can add some enhancements:

   - o **Rooms**: Allow users to join specific rooms, where only users in that room can see the messages.

     javascript

     ```javascript
     socket.emit('join room', 'room1');
     // Client sends a request to join a
     specific room
     socket.on('chat message', (msg) => {
     /* Handle message for the specific
     room */ });
     ```

o **Usernames**: Ask users to set their usernames upon logging in, and include their names with every message.

o **Typing Indicators**: Show when other users are typing in the chat.

3. **Handling Large-Scale Applications**: When building large-scale chat applications with WebSockets, you may need to consider:

o **Scalability**: Use tools like **Redis** to handle WebSocket connections across multiple servers and maintain the state of rooms or channels.

o **Persistence**: Store chat messages in a database (e.g., MongoDB or PostgreSQL) to ensure that users can retrieve old messages when they log back in.

o **Message Queues**: For large-scale applications, using message queues like **RabbitMQ** or **Kafka** can help handle high volumes of real-time messages efficiently.

In this chapter, we covered how to build real-time communication in your React and Node.js applications using **WebSockets** and **Socket.io**. We learned:

- The basics of **WebSockets** and real-time data exchange.
- How to set up **Socket.io** for bidirectional communication between the React front-end and the Node.js back-end.
- The steps to create a simple **real-time chat application**, with features like message sending and receiving in real-time.

WebSockets and Socket.io provide a robust foundation for building interactive, real-time features in your applications, opening up many possibilities for engaging user experiences such as live chats, notifications, and more.

CHAPTER 14

TESTING AND DEBUGGING YOUR APPLICATION

Writing Unit Tests for React Components Using Jest

Testing is an essential part of software development that ensures your application works as expected and prevents regressions when making changes. In this chapter, we will focus on how to write **unit tests** for your React components using **Jest**.

1. **What is Jest? Jest** is a testing framework developed by Facebook for JavaScript, and it works seamlessly with React. It allows you to run tests, check for errors, and verify that your components behave as expected. Jest comes with features like built-in

182

assertion libraries, mocks, and spies, which make testing easier.

2. **Setting Up Jest**: If you're using **Create React App**, Jest is already set up for you. If you're using a custom React setup, you can install Jest by running:

```bash
bash
```

```bash
npm install --save-dev jest
```

3. **Writing Unit Tests for a React Component**: A unit test checks the behavior of a single component in isolation. Let's write a test for a simple `Button` component.

Example of a `Button` component:

```javascript
javascript
```

```javascript
function Button({ label, onClick }) {
  return                         <button
onClick={onClick}>{label}</button>;
```

183

```
}
```

```
export default Button;
```

Now, let's write a Jest test to check if the `Button` component renders correctly and responds to user clicks.

Example of a Jest test for `Button`:

```
javascript
```

```javascript
import { render, screen, fireEvent } from
'@testing-library/react';
import Button from './Button';

test('renders button with label and handles
click event', () => {
  const handleClick = jest.fn();
  render(<Button    label="Click    Me"
onClick={handleClick} />);
```

```
// Verify button rendering

const            buttonElement            =
screen.getByText(/Click Me/i);


expect(buttonElement).toBeInTheDocument()
;


  // Simulate a click event
  fireEvent.click(buttonElement);


  // Check  if  the  onClick  handler  was
called


expect(handleClick).toHaveBeenCalledTimes
(1);
});
```

- o **render()**: Renders the component into a test environment.

- o **screen.getByText()**: Finds elements in the rendered component based on their text content.

185

o **fireEvent.click()**: Simulates a user click event.

o **expect()**: Asserts that the specified condition is true. In this case, we check if the onClick handler was called once.

4. **Running Tests**: To run the tests, use the following command:

```bash
```

```
npm test
```

Jest will find and execute any test files with the .test.js extension.

Testing Your Node.js API with Mocha and Chai

Testing your back-end API ensures that the server handles requests correctly, and that the business logic is working as expected. **Mocha** is a test framework for Node.js, and **Chai** is an assertion library that works with Mocha. Together, they provide a robust testing solution for APIs.

1. **Setting Up Mocha and Chai**: First, you need to install Mocha and Chai:

```bash
bash
```

```
npm install --save-dev mocha chai chai-http
```

- o **chai-http** is a plugin for Chai that allows you to test HTTP requests.

2. **Writing Unit Tests for Your Node.js API**: Let's say we have the following **Node.js API** route:

```javascript
javascript
```

```
app.get('/api/posts', (req, res) => {
    res.status(200).json({ message: 'List of
posts' });
});
```

Now, we'll write a test to check if this route returns the correct response.

Example of a test for the /api/posts endpoint using Mocha and Chai:

javascript

```
const chai = require('chai');
const chaiHttp = require('chai-http');
const app = require('./app');   // Your
Express app

chai.use(chaiHttp);
const { expect } = chai;

describe('GET /api/posts', () => {
  it('should return a list of posts',
(done) => {
    chai.request(app)
      .get('/api/posts')
      .end((err, res) => {
```

188

```
expect(res).to.have.status(200);
```

```
expect(res.body).to.have.property('messag
e').eql('List of posts');
        done();
    });
  });
});
```

- o **chai.request(app)**: Sends an HTTP request to the server.

- o **.get('/api/posts')**: Makes a GET request to the /api/posts endpoint.

- o **expect(res)**: Asserts the response status and body.

3. **Running the Tests**: To run the tests with Mocha, use:

```
bash
```

```
npx mocha --recursive
```

189

Mocha will execute all tests in your project.

Debugging Tips and Strategies for Both Front-End and Back-End

Debugging is an essential skill for identifying and fixing issues in your application. Below are some tips and strategies to help you debug both front-end React and back-end Node.js applications.

1. **Debugging React Applications**:

   o **Use the React Developer Tools**: The React Developer Tools browser extension allows you to inspect React component hierarchies, their state, and props. This is particularly helpful for identifying why a component is not rendering correctly.

   o **Console Logs**: Use `console.log` strategically in your components or state management to track what data is being passed around or to understand the flow of execution.

```
javascript
```

```
console.log('Component     data:',
data);
```

o **Breakpoints**: Use the built-in debugger in browsers (Chrome DevTools or Firefox Developer Tools) to set breakpoints in your JavaScript code and inspect variables or step through the code execution.

o **Error Boundaries**: In React, error boundaries catch JavaScript errors anywhere in the component tree, log those errors, and display a fallback UI. This can help in debugging issues that are otherwise hard to detect.

```javascript
class ErrorBoundary extends React.Component {
  static getDerivedStateFromError(error) {
    return { hasError: true };
  }

  componentDidCatch(error, info) {
    console.error('Error:', error, 'Info:', info);
  }

  render() {
    if (this.state.hasError) {
      return <h1>Something went wrong.</h1>;
    }
    return this.props.children;
  }
}
```

2. **Debugging Node.js Applications**:

○ **Node.js Debugger**: Node.js comes with a built-in debugger that allows you to pause code execution, inspect variables, and step through the code. To start the debugger, use:

bash

```
node inspect app.js
```

You can set breakpoints using `debugger` statements in your code:

javascript

```
debugger;
```

○ **Logging**: Use `console.log` to print out useful information like request parameters, variable values, or error messages. For more sophisticated logging, use libraries like

Winston or **Morgan** to log request details and errors.

javascript

```
const logger = require('winston');
logger.info('Informational
message');
logger.error('Error message');
```

o **Error Handling**: Use `try...catch` blocks to catch synchronous errors and proper error handling middleware in Express for asynchronous errors.

javascript

```
app.use((err, req, res, next) => {
  console.error(err.stack);
  res.status(500).send('Something
went wrong!');
});
```

194

o **External Tools**: Use **Postman** for testing API endpoints and verifying that the server responds correctly. You can also use **VS Code's built-in debugging** tools to set breakpoints and inspect your Node.js application.

In this chapter, we covered:

- **Unit testing for React** using **Jest** and **React Testing Library** to ensure your components behave as expected.

- **Testing your Node.js API** with **Mocha** and **Chai**, focusing on testing routes and handling HTTP requests.

- **Debugging strategies** for both front-end and back-end, including using browser developer tools, React DevTools, the Node.js debugger, and third-party tools like Postman and Winston.

With these tools and practices, you can ensure your applications are more reliable, easier to maintain, and free of bugs as you scale and add new features.

CHAPTER 15

DEPLOYMENT AND HOSTING

Preparing Your Application for Deployment

Before deploying your application, it's crucial to prepare it for production. This ensures that your app runs efficiently, securely, and can handle real-world traffic. In this section, we will go over the steps to prepare both your **React front-end** and **Node.js back-end** for deployment.

1. **Optimizing the React App**:

    o **Build the production-ready React app**: Use React's built-in build command to create an optimized version of your application.

    bash

    ```
    npm run build
    ```

This will create a `build/` directory containing the minified version of your app, with all assets and scripts bundled together.

o **Environment Variables**: Configure environment variables for your production environment. For example, API URLs, authentication keys, etc. You can use `.env` files to set environment variables.

bash

```
REACT_APP_API_URL=https://your-api.com
```

o **Optimizing Assets**: Make sure to optimize images, fonts, and other assets to reduce load times. Tools like **image-webpack-loader** or **react-image-optimizer** can help.

2. **Optimizing the Node.js App**:

o **Set the NODE_ENV**: In production, you should set the `NODE_ENV` variable to `"production"`, which optimizes the performance of your Node.js app.

```bash
bash

NODE_ENV=production node server.js
```

o **Database Configuration**: Ensure that your database configurations, such as connection strings or environment-specific configurations, are set up for production.

o **Error Handling and Logging**: Make sure to handle errors properly and implement logging using tools like **Winston** or **Morgan** to log important information, such as requests and errors.

3. **Security**:

- o **HTTPS**: Ensure your app uses **HTTPS** to encrypt data transferred between the client and server.

- o **Environment Variables**: Use a service like **dotenv** to load your secret keys and sensitive data securely.

- o **CORS**: Ensure Cross-Origin Resource Sharing (CORS) is set up to prevent unwanted API access.

Hosting React Apps on Platforms Like Netlify or Vercel

Once you've prepared your React app for deployment, you can host it on popular platforms like **Netlify** or **Vercel**, which offer free plans for small to medium-sized applications and are optimized for front-end apps.

1. **Hosting on Netlify**: Netlify is a powerful platform for deploying static websites and modern web apps

with continuous integration. Here's how you can deploy your React app on Netlify:

- o **Step 1: Push your code to GitHub**: Make sure your code is committed to a Git repository (GitHub, GitLab, Bitbucket, etc.).

- o **Step 2: Create a Netlify account**: Sign up for a free account at Netlify.

- o **Step 3: Connect your repository**: Once logged in, click on "New Site from Git" and choose your Git provider (e.g., GitHub).

- o **Step 4: Configure build settings**:

  - ▪ **Build Command**: `npm run build`

  - ▪ **Publish Directory**: `build`

- o **Step 5: Deploy**: Click "Deploy Site" and Netlify will automatically build and deploy your app.

Netlify also provides easy configuration for custom domains, SSL certificates, and continuous deployment (CD), so every time you push changes to your Git repository, Netlify will rebuild and redeploy your app automatically.

2. **Hosting on Vercel**: Vercel is another excellent platform for deploying React apps. It integrates seamlessly with Git repositories, making it easy to deploy and manage your front-end application.

   o **Step 1: Push your code to GitHub**: Ensure your React app is stored in a Git repository.

   o **Step 2: Create a Vercel account**: Sign up at Vercel.

   o **Step 3: Connect your repository**: After signing in, click on "New Project" and connect your GitHub account.

   o **Step 4: Configure build settings**:

      ▪ **Build Command**: `npm run build`

      ▪ **Output Directory**: `build`

   o **Step 5: Deploy**: Click "Deploy" and your React app will be live within minutes.

Vercel also automatically provides SSL certificates for HTTPS and continuous deployment, so updates are live as soon as you push changes to your repository.

Deploying Node.js Back-End on Services Like Heroku or AWS

Once your front-end is live, you'll need to deploy your back-end (Node.js) API. Two popular platforms for hosting Node.js applications are **Heroku** and **AWS** (Amazon Web Services).

1. **Deploying Node.js on Heroku**: Heroku is a platform-as-a-service (PaaS) that simplifies the deployment and scaling of Node.js applications.

   o **Step 1: Install the Heroku CLI**: Download and install the Heroku CLI from here.

o **Step 2: Log in to Heroku**: Open your terminal and log in to your Heroku account.

bash

```
heroku login
```

o **Step 3: Create a new Heroku app**:

bash

```
heroku create
```

o **Step 4: Set up Git**: Initialize a Git repository if you haven't already.

bash

```
git init
git add .
git commit -m "Initial commit"
```

o **Step 5: Deploy the app**:

```
bash
```

```
git push heroku master
```

- ○ **Step 6: Set up environment variables**: On Heroku, you can configure environment variables using the CLI or the dashboard.

```
bash
```

```
heroku                   config:set
NODE_ENV=production
```

- ○ **Step 7: Open your app**: Once the deployment is complete, Heroku will provide a URL for your app.

```
bash
```

```
heroku open
```

2. Heroku simplifies the deployment process by managing infrastructure, scaling, and provisioning

205

servers for you, which makes it a great option for small to medium-sized applications.

3. **Deploying Node.js on AWS (Amazon Web Services)**: AWS provides more control and flexibility, but it requires more configuration. One popular service for hosting Node.js applications is **AWS EC2** (Elastic Compute Cloud), which allows you to run virtual servers.

  o **Step 1: Set up an AWS account**: Sign up for an AWS account at <u>AWS</u>.

  o **Step 2: Launch an EC2 instance**:

    ▪ In the AWS Management Console, go to EC2 and launch a new instance.

    ▪ Select an appropriate machine (e.g., **Amazon Linux 2** or **Ubuntu**).

    ▪ Create and download an SSH key pair for accessing your instance.

  o **Step 3: Connect to the EC2 instance**:

- Use SSH to connect to your EC2 instance:

```bash
ssh -i your-key.pem ec2-user@your-ec2-public-ip
```

o **Step 4: Install Node.js**:

- Update the system and install Node.js:

```bash
sudo yum update -y
sudo yum install nodejs -y
```

o **Step 5: Upload your application**:

- You can upload your Node.js app using SCP or Git.
- For example, using Git:

```bash
```

```
git                           clone
https://github.com/your-
repo.git
cd your-repo
```

o **Step 6: Start the Node.js server**:

```bash
```

```
node server.js
```

o **Step 7: Set up a reverse proxy**: To serve your Node.js application via HTTP, configure a reverse proxy with **Nginx** or **Apache** to forward requests to your Node.js app.

o **Step 8: Open security groups**: Ensure that your EC2 security group allows traffic on port 80 (HTTP) and 443 (HTTPS).

AWS provides more control over your infrastructure, which is ideal for larger applications that need scalability and more customization.

In this chapter, we covered the steps for deploying and hosting both the **React front-end** and **Node.js back-end**:

- **React deployment**: We covered how to deploy React apps on **Netlify** and **Vercel**, both of which provide free plans with features like continuous deployment, custom domains, and SSL certificates.

- **Node.js back-end deployment**: We explored **Heroku**, which offers a simple PaaS solution, and **AWS EC2**, which provides more control and scalability for larger applications.

By following these steps, you can efficiently deploy and host your full-stack applications, allowing them to scale and serve real-world traffic.

CHAPTER 16

CONTINUOUS INTEGRATION AND CONTINUOUS DEPLOYMENT (CI/CD)

Introduction to CI/CD Pipelines

Continuous Integration (CI) and **Continuous Deployment (CD)** are essential practices in modern software development that help streamline development workflows, ensure code quality, and enable faster releases.

1. **What is CI/CD?**

    o **Continuous Integration (CI)** refers to the practice of automatically integrating code changes from multiple contributors into a shared repository several times a day. Every change made by developers is automatically built and tested, ensuring that the code works correctly and reducing the chances of integration errors.

- o **Continuous Deployment (CD)** goes hand in hand with CI. After a successful build and test, CD automates the process of deploying the application to production. This ensures that the latest code is always deployed with minimal human intervention.

2. **Why Implement CI/CD?**

- o **Faster releases**: With automated pipelines, code can be released more frequently and reliably.

- o **Improved code quality**: Every code change is automatically tested, reducing bugs and errors.

- o **Automation**: Repetitive tasks like building, testing, and deploying are automated, saving developers time and reducing the chance of human error.

- o **Consistency**: CI/CD pipelines ensure that the same process is followed every time a change is made.

212

Automating Tests, Builds, and Deployments

The core concept of CI/CD is automation. Let's look at how to automate three essential steps in your development workflow:

1. **Automating Tests**: In a CI pipeline, the first step is to run your automated tests to ensure that the code is functioning as expected. This could include:

    o **Unit tests**: Ensure that individual functions or components work correctly.

    o **Integration tests**: Check that different parts of the application work together as expected.

    o **End-to-end tests**: Test the entire application flow to ensure the system behaves as a whole.

In practice, whenever code is pushed to the repository, an automated process will run these tests. If any test fails, the pipeline stops, and developers are notified to fix the issue before merging the code into the main branch.

Example of a simple test setup:

```bash
```

```
npm test
```

2. **Automating Builds**: Once the tests pass, the next step is to automate the build process. For React applications, this means running a build command to create the optimized production version of the app.

Example:

```bash
```

```
npm run build
```

For Node.js back-end applications, this could involve bundling and optimizing server code, handling environment configurations, and ensuring that all dependencies are correctly installed.

3. **Automating Deployments**: After a successful build, the final step in the CI/CD pipeline is to automatically deploy the code to the staging or production environment. This can be done using deployment tools that integrate with your version control system, like **Heroku**, **Netlify**, **AWS**, or **Docker**.

Example of deployment in a pipeline:

```bash
bash
```

```bash
npm run deploy
```

In the CI/CD pipeline, the process of deploying to staging and production environments is triggered automatically after the build is successful.

215

To implement CI/CD, we use services that manage the pipeline for us. Some of the most popular services are **GitHub Actions** and **Jenkins**. These services allow you to define and automate the entire CI/CD pipeline.

1. **GitHub Actions**: GitHub Actions is a feature within GitHub that allows you to automate your workflows, including CI/CD processes. It is deeply integrated with GitHub, so it is a great choice for projects hosted on GitHub.

   Setting up GitHub Actions:

   o To get started with GitHub Actions, create a `.github/workflows/` directory in your repository and add a YAML file (e.g., `ci-cd-`

216

`pipeline.yml`) to define the steps of your pipeline.

Example GitHub Actions YAML file:

```yaml
name: CI/CD Pipeline

on:
  push:
    branches:
      - main

jobs:
  build:
    runs-on: ubuntu-latest
    steps:
      - name: Checkout code
        uses: actions/checkout@v2

      - name: Set up Node.js
        uses: actions/setup-node@v2
```

```
      with:

         node-version: '14'


      - name: Install dependencies

        run: npm install


      - name: Run tests

        run: npm test


      - name: Build the React app

        run: npm run build


      - name: Deploy to Netlify

        run: npm run deploy

        env:

          NETLIFY_AUTH_TOKEN:          ${{
secrets.NETLIFY_AUTH_TOKEN }}

          NETLIFY_SITE_ID:             ${{
secrets.NETLIFY_SITE_ID }}
```

Key points:

- o `on: push`: This triggers the pipeline whenever code is pushed to the `main` branch.

- o `jobs`: Defines the steps of the pipeline (checkout code, set up Node.js, install dependencies, run tests, build the app, and deploy).

- o `NETLIFY_AUTH_TOKEN` and `NETLIFY_SITE_ID` are stored as GitHub secrets to keep them secure.

Once the action is set up, every time you push changes to GitHub, GitHub Actions will automatically run the tests, build the app, and deploy it to Netlify.

2. **Jenkins**: Jenkins is an open-source automation server used for continuous integration and continuous delivery. Jenkins allows you to automate the build, test, and deployment processes through pipelines.

Setting up Jenkins:

- o Install Jenkins on your server and create a new job (or pipeline) in Jenkins.

- o Define the steps of your pipeline in a Jenkinsfile, which is stored in your repository.

Example Jenkinsfile:

```groovy
groovy


pipeline {
  agent any


  stages {
    stage('Install dependencies') {
      steps {
        script {
          sh 'npm install'

        }

      }

    }
```

```
stage('Run tests') {

  steps {

    script {

      sh 'npm test'

    }

  }

}


stage('Build app') {

  steps {

    script {

      sh 'npm run build'

    }

  }

}


stage('Deploy') {

  steps {

    script {

      sh 'npm run deploy'

    }
```

221

```
        }

      }

    }

  }
```

Key points:

- o **Stages**: Defines the different stages of your pipeline (install dependencies, run tests, build, deploy).

- o **Script**: Jenkins executes each step using shell commands (e.g., `sh 'npm install'`).

Jenkins provides flexibility for large-scale projects and custom workflows, but it requires more configuration and infrastructure compared to services like GitHub Actions.

In this chapter, we've explored the fundamentals of **CI/CD** (Continuous Integration and Continuous Deployment) and how to set up automated pipelines for your React and Node.js applications.

- **CI/CD Pipelines**: Automate the process of testing, building, and deploying your applications, improving development efficiency, and ensuring higher code quality.
- **GitHub Actions**: An easy-to-use service integrated with GitHub that automates your workflows and CI/CD pipeline.
- **Jenkins**: A more customizable solution for CI/CD that allows for complex workflows and can be integrated with various services.

By implementing CI/CD, you can continuously deliver features, fix bugs, and deploy your applications more efficiently, ensuring that your development process remains smooth and scalable.

CHAPTER 17

ADVANCED FEATURES AND BEST PRACTICES

Using Redux for State Management in Large Applications

As React applications grow in size and complexity, managing state across multiple components can become challenging. **Redux** is a popular state management library that helps manage application state in a predictable way, making it easier to handle state across large and complex React applications.

1. **Why Use Redux?**

    o **Centralized State**: Redux stores the entire state of the application in a single **store**, making it easier to manage state changes and access data throughout your app.

o **Predictable State Management**: Redux enforces a predictable flow of state updates, which makes it easier to debug and maintain.

o **Separation of Concerns**: By separating state management from UI components, Redux promotes a clean architecture.

2. **Core Concepts of Redux**:

o **Store**: The central repository of the application state.

o **Actions**: Plain JavaScript objects that describe what happened. Actions are dispatched to indicate that something has changed in the app.

o **Reducers**: Pure functions that specify how the state changes in response to actions. They take the current state and the action, and return a new state.

o **Dispatch**: A function that sends actions to the store, triggering state updates.

o **Selectors**: Functions that help retrieve parts of the state from the store.

225

3. **Setting Up Redux**: To get started with Redux, you'll need to install the necessary libraries:

```bash
npm install redux react-redux
```

- **Creating the Store**:

```javascript
import { createStore } from 'redux';

// Initial state
const initialState = {
  user: null,
};

// Reducer function
const rootReducer = (state =
initialState, action) => {
  switch (action.type) {
    case 'SET_USER':
```

```
        return    {   ...state,   user:
action.payload };
    default:
      return state;
  }
};
```

```
// Create Redux store
const            store            =
createStore(rootReducer);
```

o **Connecting Redux to React**: To access the Redux store in your React components, use the `Provider` component from `react-redux` to make the store available to the entire app.

```
javascript
```

```
import React from 'react';
import { Provider } from 'react-redux';
import { render } from 'react-dom';
```

```
import App from './App';


render(

  <Provider store={store}>

    <App />

  </Provider>,

  document.getElementById('root')

);
```

o **Dispatching Actions**: In your components, use the `useDispatch` hook to dispatch actions to update the state.

javascript

```
import { useDispatch } from 'react-redux';


function LoginButton() {
  const dispatch = useDispatch();


  const handleLogin = () => {
```

```
    const user = { name: 'John Doe'
};

    dispatch({   type:   'SET_USER',
payload: user });
    };


    return              <button
onClick={handleLogin}>Login</button
>;

    }
```

o **Accessing State**: Use the `useSelector` hook to access parts of the state in your components.

```
javascript


import { useSelector } from 'react-
redux';


function UserProfile() {
```

```
const  user  =  useSelector((state)
=> state.user);


if (!user) {

    return <div>Please log in</div>;

}


return                <div>Welcome,
{user.name}</div>;

}
```

4. **Best Practices for Using Redux**:

    o **Keep reducers pure**: A reducer should not
       mutate the state or have side effects.

    o **Modularize your state**: Organize the state into
       logical chunks to make it easier to manage (e.g.,
       user, posts, auth).

    o **Use action creators**: Instead of manually
       dispatching actions in components, define action
       creators to improve maintainability.

230

o **Leverage middleware**: Use middleware like **redux-thunk** for handling async actions.

Code Splitting and Lazy Loading to Improve Performance

In large React applications, **code splitting** and **lazy loading** are essential strategies for improving performance. These techniques help reduce the initial load time by loading only the necessary code when needed.

1. **Code Splitting**: Code splitting allows you to break your application into smaller, more manageable chunks. This can be done at the component level, enabling you to load parts of the app on demand instead of loading everything at once.

   o **React.lazy()**: React provides a built-in function called `React.lazy()` to load components dynamically.

   ```javascript
   ```

```
const LazyComponent = React.lazy(()
=> import('./LazyComponent'));

function App() {
  return (
    <Suspense
fallback={<div>Loading...</div>}>
      <LazyComponent />
    </Suspense>
  );
}
```

- **React.lazy()**: Dynamically imports the component only when it's needed.

- **Suspense**: Wraps the lazy-loaded component and shows a fallback UI (like a loading spinner) until the component is loaded.

232

2. **Dynamic Imports**: You can split the code based on different routes using React Router. For example, load route components only when they are visited.

Example of dynamic imports with **React Router**:

```javascript
import React, { Suspense } from 'react';
import { BrowserRouter as Router, Route, Switch } from 'react-router-dom';

const Home = React.lazy(() => import('./Home'));
const About = React.lazy(() => import('./About'));

function App() {
  return (
    <Router>
      <Suspense fallback={<div>Loading...</div>}>
```

233

```
        <Switch>

            <Route      exact       path="/"
component={Home} />

            <Route              path="/about"
component={About} />

        </Switch>

      </Suspense>

    </Router>

  );

}


export default App;
```

3. **Webpack and Code Splitting**: If you are using **Webpack**, code splitting is easy to implement. Webpack automatically splits the code into separate bundles based on your dynamic imports or entry points.

4. **Optimizing Performance with Lazy Loading**: Lazy loading ensures that the app loads faster by loading only the essential code and deferring the rest.

This is particularly useful for large React applications with many routes or components.

Implementing Server-Side Rendering (SSR) with React

Server-Side Rendering (SSR) is a technique where React renders the initial HTML of your application on the server before sending it to the browser. This improves the initial loading time and SEO (Search Engine Optimization) because the content is ready when the page loads, rather than having to wait for JavaScript to load and render the content.

1. **Why Use SSR?**

   o **Faster initial load**: The server sends a fully rendered HTML page to the browser, so the user can see the content immediately.

   o **Improved SEO**: Search engines can crawl the content on the server-rendered page, improving the app's SEO ranking.

- o **Better performance**: By offloading rendering to the server, the client has less work to do, improving performance for slower devices.

2. **Setting Up SSR in React**: To enable SSR in React, you'll need to use **ReactDOMServer** for rendering React components on the server.

   - o **Step 1: Create a server using Express**: You'll need to create a Node.js server using **Express** to handle SSR.

     javascript

     ```javascript
     import express from 'express';
     import React from 'react';
     import ReactDOMServer from 'react-dom/server';
     import App from './App';

     const app = express();
     ```

```
app.use(express.static('public'));

// Serve static assets


app.get('*', (req, res) => {

  const            content            =

ReactDOMServer.renderToString(<App

/>);


  res.send(`

    <!DOCTYPE html>

    <html>

      <head>

        <title>SSR            with

React</title>

      </head>

      <body>

        <div

id="root">${content}</div>

        <script

src="bundle.js"></script> <!-- Your

bundled JavaScript -->

      </body>
```

```
    </html>

    `);

});


app.listen(3000, () => {

  console.log('Server    running    on

port 3000');

});
```

3. **Webpack for SSR**: To set up SSR with Webpack, you need to configure Webpack to bundle the server-side and client-side code separately. This typically involves:

   o **Server-side Webpack configuration**: You will create a separate Webpack configuration to bundle the server code for SSR.

   o **Client-side Webpack configuration**: A different configuration for the client-side JavaScript bundle.

4. **React Hydration**: After the server sends the pre-rendered HTML to the browser, React needs to

"hydrate" the page, which means it attaches event listeners and prepares the page for interaction.

Example of hydration:

javascript

```
import React from 'react';
import ReactDOM from 'react-dom';
import App from './App';

ReactDOM.hydrate(
  <App />,
  document.getElementById('root')
);
```

5. **SSR with Frameworks**: Several frameworks make implementing SSR with React easier, including **Next.js**. These frameworks handle the complexity of SSR out of the box, offering features like automatic code splitting, routing, and server-side rendering.

239

In this chapter, we covered advanced features and best practices for building scalable and high-performance applications:

- **Using Redux**: We explored how Redux helps with state management in large applications by centralizing state and ensuring predictable updates.

- **Code Splitting and Lazy Loading**: These techniques allow us to split the code into smaller chunks, improving the initial load time and overall performance.

- **Implementing SSR**: Server-Side Rendering (SSR) provides faster initial loading and better SEO by rendering content on the server before sending it to the client.

By implementing these techniques, you can build applications that are more efficient, maintainable, and optimized for performance and scalability.

CHAPTER 18

FINAL PROJECT – BUILDING A FULL-STACK WEB APP

Putting Everything Together: Building a Fully Functional Web App

from Scratch

In this chapter, we will apply everything we've learned to build a fully functional **full-stack web app** from scratch using **React** for the front-end and **Node.js** for the back-end. By the end of this chapter, you will have a working application, complete with state management, routing, authentication, database integration, and deployment.

Overview of the Full-Stack Web App: Let's assume we are building a **task management app** where users can:

- Register and log in to the application.
- Create, view, and manage tasks.

- Organize tasks by categories and set deadlines.

- Communicate in real-time through a chat feature.

This app will require both a front-end and a back-end, as well as **authentication**, **database integration**, and **real-time communication**. We'll break it down step-by-step.

Step-by-Step Guidance on Building a Real-World Application with React and Node.js

1. **Setting Up the Project Structure**:

   o **Front-End (React)**: Start by creating a React app using Create React App:

   bash

   ```
   npx create-react-app task-manager-client
   cd task-manager-client
   ```

   Install the necessary libraries:

```
bash
```

```
npm install axios react-router-dom
redux react-redux
```

o **Back-End (Node.js)**: Create a directory for the back-end:

```
bash
```

```
mkdir task-manager-server
cd task-manager-server
```

Initialize a Node.js project and install the required dependencies:

```
bash
```

```
npm init -y
npm    install    express    mongoose
bcryptjs jsonwebtoken socket.io
```

2. **Building the Front-End**:

244

o **Routing with React Router**: Set up routing in `App.js` to handle different pages (e.g., Home, Login, Dashboard).

```javascript
import { BrowserRouter as Router,
Route, Switch } from 'react-router-
dom';
import Home from './pages/Home';
import Login from './pages/Login';
import Dashboard from
'./pages/Dashboard';

function App() {
  return (
    <Router>
      <Switch>
        <Route path="/" exact
component={Home} />
        <Route path="/login"
component={Login} />
```

245

```
      <Route      path="/dashboard"
component={Dashboard} />
      </Switch>
    </Router>
  );
}
```

o **Managing State with Redux**: Create actions and reducers to manage tasks, user authentication, and settings.

```javascript
// actions/taskActions.js
export const addTask = (task) => ({
  type: 'ADD_TASK',
  payload: task,
});


// reducers/taskReducer.js
const taskReducer = (state = [],
action) => {
```

```
switch (action.type) {

  case 'ADD_TASK':

    return              [...state,

action.payload];

  default:

    return state;

}

};
```

o **User Authentication**: Use **JWT** (JSON Web Tokens) for user authentication. The login page should allow users to submit their credentials, validate them, and store the token in local storage.

```javascript

import axios from 'axios';

const handleLogin = async (e) => {
  e.preventDefault();
```

247

```
  const    response    =    await
axios.post('/api/login', { username,
password });
  localStorage.setItem('token',
response.data.token);
};
```

3. **Building the Back-End**:

   o **Setting Up Express Server**: In your `task-manager-server` directory, set up a basic Express server.

   javascript

   ```
const express = require('express');
const         mongoose         =
require('mongoose');
const cors = require('cors');

const app = express();
app.use(cors());
app.use(express.json());
   ```

```
mongoose.connect('mongodb://localho
st:27017/taskmanager',             {
useNewUrlParser:              true,
useUnifiedTopology: true })
  .then(()  =>  console.log('MongoDB
connected'))
  .catch(err => console.log(err));


// Basic route
app.get('/', (req, res) => {
  res.send('Welcome to Task Manager
API');
});


app.listen(5000,          ()         =>
console.log('Server running on port
5000'));
```

o **Setting Up User Authentication**: Create a
  User model with **bcrypt** for password

hashing and **jsonwebtoken** for token generation.

```javascript
const bcrypt = require('bcryptjs');
const jwt = require('jsonwebtoken');
const User = mongoose.model('User',
{ username: String, password: String
});


app.post('/api/login', async (req,
res) => {
  const { username, password } =
req.body;
  const user = await User.findOne({
username });

  if            (!user            ||
!bcrypt.compareSync(password,
user.password)) {
```

```
      return      res.status(401).json({

message: 'Invalid credentials' });

   }


   const token = jwt.sign({ userId:

user._id }, 'secret', { expiresIn:

'1h' });

   res.json({ token });

});
```

o **Setting Up Task Model**: Define a `Task`
model where each task can have a title,
description, deadline, and assigned user.

```
javascript


const Task = mongoose.model('Task',

{

  title: String,

  description: String,

  deadline: Date,
```

251

```
userId:

mongoose.Schema.Types.ObjectId,

});
```

4. **Connecting Front-End and Back-End**:

   o **Making API Requests**: Use **Axios** to interact with your back-end API for tasks and user authentication.

   ```javascript
   const fetchTasks = async () => {
     const token = localStorage.getItem('token');
     const response = await axios.get('/api/tasks', {
       headers: { Authorization: `Bearer ${token}` },
     });
     setTasks(response.data);
   };
   ```

o **Real-Time Features with WebSockets**:
Implement **Socket.io** to handle real-time
updates for tasks (e.g., when a task is updated
or completed by another user).

Server-side (Node.js):

```javascript
const socketIo =
require('socket.io');
const io = socketIo(server);

io.on('connection', (socket) => {
  console.log('User connected');
  socket.on('taskUpdated', (task) =>
{

socket.broadcast.emit('taskUpdated'
, task);  // Send to all other users
  });
});
```

253

Client-side (React):

javascript

```
const              socket             =
io('http://localhost:5000');
socket.on('taskUpdated', (task) => {
  setTasks(prevTasks              =>
[...prevTasks, task]);
});
```

Final Tips on Scaling, Performance Optimization, and Future Enhancements

1. **Scaling**:

   o **Back-End**: For scaling Node.js, consider using a **cluster** module to take advantage of multi-core systems. This will help handle more requests efficiently by running multiple instances of your app.

- o **Front-End**: For scaling React, ensure that components are reusable and consider using **React.memo** and **useMemo** to prevent unnecessary re-renders.

- o **Database**: If your app grows, use database optimization techniques like **indexing**, **pagination**, and **caching**.

2. **Performance Optimization**:

    - o **Lazy Loading**: Use **React.lazy** for code splitting to load only the components required for the initial page render.

    - o **Image Optimization**: Use libraries like **image-webpack-loader** to optimize images before serving them.

    - o **API Caching**: Use caching mechanisms like **Redis** for frequently accessed data, such as task lists or user profiles.

3. **Future Enhancements**:

o **Authentication**: Add **OAuth** or **JWT refresh tokens** to improve security and user experience for long sessions.

o **Mobile Optimization**: Consider using **React Native** to create a mobile version of the task manager app.

o **Progressive Web App (PWA)**: Convert the app into a PWA to allow users to use the app offline and get push notifications.

o **Microservices**: Break the back-end into smaller services (e.g., separate user authentication, task management, and real-time features).

In this chapter, we successfully built a **full-stack web application** using **React** for the front-end and **Node.js** for the back-end. We integrated **Redux** for state management, implemented **real-time communication** with **Socket.io**, and learned how to deploy and manage our app.

We also discussed:

- **Scaling** and **optimizing performance** for large applications.
- **Future enhancements** to take your app to the next level.

By following this step-by-step guide, you now have a fully functional, full-stack web app ready for further development and deployment.